STAIRWAY
13

© Paul Collier and Donald S. Taylor 2007

Published by The Bluecoat Press, Liverpool
Book design by MARCH Graphic Design Studio, Liverpool
Printed by Compass Press

Cover photograph courtesy of Empics Ltd
Photograph on page 104 courtesy of Reuters

ISBN 978 904438 47 2

ACKNOWLEDGEMENTS
We would like to thank the following for their help and inspiration in the writing of this
book – Rodger Baillie, Stuart Bolton, Marion Collier, Michael Crick, David Drage, Shane
Fenton and the 'Glenrothes Gazette', Roddy Forsyth, 'The Herald', (Glasgow), Allan Herron,
Phil Hughes, Mike Kelly, Tommy Malcolm, 'Mirror Group Newspapers', Iain McCartney,
John McClelland, Ian Paul, Rangers Football Club, 'The Scottish Sun', Peter Semple.

Special thanks to John Burrowes
for allowing us to use extracts from his book 'Frontline Report'.

A donation from the proceeds of the sale of this book will be given to the
Eastpark Children's Home, Maryhill, Glasgow.

STAIRWAY 13

THE STORY OF THE 1971 IBROX DISASTER

PAUL COLLIER
DONALD S. TAYLOR

THE BLUECOAT PRESS

This book is dedicated to the memory of the Rangers supporters who lost their lives on 2 January 1971.

George Adams (43), Clydebank
Hugh Addie (33), Barrhead
David Anderson (45), Easterhouse
Richard Barke (15), Shettleston
John Buchanan (37), Castlemilk
Robert Cairns (17), Edinburgh
Robert Carrigan (13), Kirkintilloch
John Crawford (23), Springburn
Thomas Dickson (32), Airdrie
Charles Dougan (31), Clydebank
Francis Dover (16), Possilpark
David Duff (23), Possil
Peter Easton (13), Markinch
Peter Farries (26), Sandyhills
Margaret Ferguson (18), Falkirk
George Findlay (21), Townhead
Ian Frew (21), Airdrie
John Gardiner (32), Knightswood
Robert Grant (21), Bishopton
Thomas Grant (16), Yoker
James Gray (37), Larkhall
Adam Henderson (43), Cumbernauld
Ian Hunter (14), Newmains
Brian Hutchison (16), Barlanark
George Irwin (22), Dunoon
John Jeffrey (16), Yoker
Andrew Lindsay (18), Easterhouse
Charles Griffiths Livingston (30), Tollcross, Glasgow
James Mair (19), Larkhall
Russell Malcolm (16), Broxburn
Robert Maxwell (15), Blantyre
Thomas Melville (17), Possil
Thomas Morgan (14), Bearsden

Douglas Morrison (15), Markinch
Robert Mulholland (16), Drumchapel
Robert McAdam (36), Denny
Duncan McBrearty (17), Shettleston
David McGhee (14), Bearsden
James McGovern (24), Tranent
Alex McIntyre (29), Barrhead
John McLeay (23), Slammanan
Richard McLeay (28), Slammanan
Donald McPherson (30), Craigton
Thomas McRobbie (17), Bridgeton
John Neil (29), Shettleston
Alexander Orr (16), Airdrie
Martin Paton (14), Markinch
Mason Phillips (14), Markinch
Nigel Pickup (9), Liverpool
James Rae (19), Kirkintilloch
Robert Rae (25), Patrick
Walter Raeburn (36), Broughton
Matthew Reid (49), Caldercruix
John Semple (18), Kirkintilloch
William Shaw (38), Ruchazie
Walter Shields (15), Springburn
James Sibbald (28), Restalrig
George Smith (40), Cardonald
William Somerhill (17), Gallowgate, Glasgow
Charles Stirling (20), Chapelhall
Thomas Stirling (16), Kirkintilloch
Donald Sutherland (14), Bearsden
Brian Todd (14), Markinch
James Trainer (20), Bridgeton
George Wilson (15), Greenock
Peter Wright (31), Uddingston

CONTENTS

GEORGE BEST
(Manchester United & Northern Ireland)

The great game of football continues to give millions of people the world over enormous pleasure, be it as a participant or as a spectator sport. I know I was lucky to gain tremendous satisfaction from playing a game which I was born to love.

Unfortunately, over the years there has been a darker side to football which has seen some horrendous tragedies associated with the game. I can remember my own club, Manchester United, still recovering from the aftermath of the Munich aircrash when I joined as an amateur in 1961. The terrible event three years earlier claimed the lives of players, officials and journalists alike.

There have been many tragedies which have involved supporters losing their lives in dreadful accidents. The Ibrox Disaster of 1971 is one such tragedy which springs to mind when 66 supporters lost their lives at the end of an Old Firm game. Many years have passed since that awful day but the events remain prominent in the memory for those old enough to recollect it.

I remember gladly accepting an invitation to play in a benefit game for the dependants of those who had perished in the Ibrox Disaster. The game I recall was played at Hampden Park a few weeks after the tragedy. I was delighted to play my small part in helping to boost the Disaster fund which had been set up in the wake of the events of 2 January 1971.

The pages which follow endeavour to tell the story of the Ibrox Disaster as it happened. Hopefully it will stand as a fitting tribute to those Rangers supporters who lost their lives that day supporting their team.

PREFACE

The second day of January 1971 will remain a date indelibly etched in the memory of Rangers supporters. It is a date, however, which recounts not feelings of euphoria and triumph but emotions of deep sorrow and terrible sadness. More than 36 years have passed since that fateful day on which 66 Rangers supporters lost their lives in the most tragic of circumstances and yet its very mention still causes a chilling shudder three decades on. The Ibrox Disaster remains the worst tragedy to occur at a Scottish football match and the second worst to happen at a British stadium. Fatalities and injury though have sadly occurred at football games for almost as long as supporters have been attending them.

On 9 March 1946, 33 people perished and approximately 500 were hurt at an FA Cup quarterfinal tie between Bolton Wanderers and Stoke City at Burnden Park. Supporters turned up in their droves, many to see the incomparable Stanley Matthews, yet, tragically, serious overcrowding caused two crush barriers at the Railway End of the ground to collapse. Sadly, many fans were suffocated. The official report in the wake of the accident depicted Bolton's ground as being 'typical of most leading football grounds'[1] and added that the disaster 'might easily be repeated at 20 or 30 other grounds.'[2] The scathing declaration suggested that the government should announce laws to require clubs to license their grounds. Additionally, the report declared that an accurate method of counting crowds was required to limit each section of the grounds and so prevent overcrowding. Sadly, this recommendation was not heeded.

Tragedy struck on several occasions during the 1980s, a decade which put crowd safety under the spotlight like never before. On 11 May 1985, Bradford City's promotion celebrations were marred in a horrendous way. At their game against Lincoln City, the main stand became engulfed in fire, which swept at frightening speed through the timber construction. Supporters tried desperately to escape the embracing flames, which were fuelled by strong winds but many became trapped and unable to flee the panic. More than 150 fans were ferried to hospital, some suffering from severe burns. The stand which had been built in 1908 had been due to be refurbished after that final home game of the 1984/85 season but such plans proved too late for the 56 people who lost their lives. The cause of the accident was attributed to a lighted cigarette falling through a gap in a floorboard and setting alight a large quantity of rubbish which had gathered beneath the stand over many years. Alarm was also expressed that exit gates at the back of the main stand at Valley Parade had remained padlocked, which prevented escape. On that same day, a further tragedy occurred when a young boy died at St Andrews – home of Birmingham City – when a wall collapsed during a riot by visiting Leeds United supporters. These tragic events, however, were to be followed by more loss of life 18 days later.

The European Cup Final of 29 May 1985, played in the Heysel Stadium, Brussels, brought further death and injury. Supporters of the two finalists – Liverpool and Juventus – had been placed adjacent to each other when fighting broke out between the two groups. The players had not taken to the field when commotion began as fans viciously charged each other across the terraces. Many Italian fans who attempted to escape the trouble were forced against a wall, which duly collapsed under pressure causing the deaths of 39 people.

The official reports into the Heysel Stadium and Bradford City disasters highlighted neglect of their grounds by the respective clubs who, it appeared, were keener to bolster their teams with fresh playing talent rather than spending the money on ground improvements. In the wake of the Bradford disaster, annual ground safety inspections were announced as well as a total ban on smoking in wooden stands. More drastic action though was to be announced four years later following the most appalling loss of life ever at a British sporting venue.

When Liverpool met Nottingham Forest in a FA Cup Semi-final tie at Sheffield Wednesday's home ground – Hillsborough – on 15 April 1989, no one could have envisaged the chaos, which would precede the kick-off that afternoon. Crowd congestion outside the Leppings Lane turnstiles had reached a critical level whereupon the police ordered an exit gate to be opened to help alleviate the crush outside the ground. Liverpool supporters headed for the central terracing pens, which were already crowded. No attempt was made to direct fans to the quieter side-pens and, as a result, two crush barriers collapsed under the weight of bodies which occupied that section. Ninety-five people perished due to the sheer weight of numbers although the death toll was to rise to 96 when one fan died several years later in hospital. Lord Justice Taylor's report which followed was highly critical of those running football as he declared, 'the safety of those on the terraces has not been a priority'[3] and added that it was 'depressing and chastening'[4] that the prior official reports on crowd safety, most of which had followed disasters, had not been acted upon. Taylor recommended that grounds should be made all-seater and terraces abolished.

Football has a daunting and unwanted list of tragedies to its name which have occurred around the globe. Numerous supporters have lost their lives supporting their teams. 340 fans were crushed to death on icy terraces during a UEFA Cup tie between Spartak Moscow and Haarlem in the Lenin Stadium, Moscow on 20 October 1982 and just 20 fewer lost their lives at a football stadium in Lima, Peru on 24 May 1964 at an international match against Argentina. During a riot at a ground in Buenos Aires on 23 May 1968, 73 people were killed while two further tragedies occurred in the late 1980s. On 12 March 1988, 80 people lost their lives at a football stadium in Kathmandu, Nepal following a stampede and a further 83 people perished in a similar manner on 15 April 1989, at a football venue in Guatemala City. More loss of life was to happen at football stadia at the turn of the century. On 11 April 2001, a match between South African rivals Kaiser Chiefs and Orlando Pirates had attracted a capacity crowd of 62,000 spectators. Thousands of ticketless fans at the Ellis Park stadium in Johannesburg though, broke down fencing and stormed the already packed arena. During the ensuing stampede, 14 people were killed outside the ground, 29 killed inside and more that 155 others were injured. Eighteen days later, at a football match in Lumbashi in the Democratic Republic of Congo, eight people were killed and 51 seriously injured during rioting between rival supporters in a game between Lupopo and Mazembe. On 9 May 2001, some 100 people died during a stampede at a game in Accra, Ghana between the country's top two sides – Hearts of Oak and Asante Kotoke.

Attention though, returns to Scotland where during a match at Shawfield in 1957 between Clyde and Celtic, part of a concrete retaining barrier gave way, which resulted in a young boy losing his life.

It is Ibrox, though, which has had the misfortune to bear testament to several calamities, which have occurred at Rangers home ground. On 3 April 1902, Ibrox was chosen to host the international fixture between Scotland and England. The stadium gates were opened some three hours before kick-off in anticipation of accommodating the vast numbers of spectators who were expected to attend the game. Before commencement of the match, the terracing on the southwest side of the ground was solidly packed, although more spectators attempted to gain entry though the gangways at the top of the terracing were heavily congested. Several minutes into the game, a section of the rear terracing collapsed and hundreds of spectators plunged into a 40 feet chasm. Tragically, many fell to their deaths. Doctors treated several hundred people while the referee abandoned the game, which had attracted a crowd of 75,000. Sadly, many of those who attended the game were oblivious to the seriousness of the incident, as attention remained focussed on the match itself, which stood at 1-1 before it was stopped.

This first Ibrox disaster was to claim the lives of 25 spectators although some of this number did not perish at the ground but died later at hospital from injuries which they had sustained. The stadium at this time had been less than three years old, although some individuals had held grave reservations about the strength and quality of the wooden terracing before the accident occurred. The infamous Stairway 13, located in the northeast corner of Rangers huge Ibrox stadium gained unwanted notoriety for three accidents, which happened prior to the horrific incident of 1971. On 16 September 1961, two supporters stumbled and then fell on the steep Stairway when exiting the stadium after a 2-2 draw with Glasgow 'Old Firm' rivals, Celtic. Fans who were behind those who had fallen attempted to avoid treading on their fellow supporters. However, during the resulting bedlam, the central wooden barrier, which divided the Stairway, shattered under the strain. Additionally, the right hand perimeter picket fence also gave way due to the pressure although this paradoxically, aided the escape of some supporters. Other fans were not so lucky in avoiding the crush as 44 people were injured in the chaos whilst two others, sadly, lost their lives. The 1961 incident resulted in the single central wooden barrier being replaced by six tubular steel 'spines', which ran the full length of the Stairway and in so doing, divided it into seven narrower lanes. The rationale behind this change was that it would break up the flow of spectators, causing those leaving the stadium to do so in a more orderly fashion. Significantly, the outer perimeter picket surround was replaced by reinforced fencing. Tragically, the implementation of such barriers was to have a dramatic bearing on events less than ten years later. On 11 September 1967, however, another incident was to occur on the same Stairway when a supporter lost his footing following a match once again against rivals Celtic. On this occasion, 11 people were hurt. Finally, on 2 January 1969, at the end of a further game between the Glasgow giants, 30 people suffered injury close to the bottom of exit 13 when an individual again stumbled, causing those behind to fall. Following the final incident of the decade on Stairway 13, safety officers recommended that open railings should replace the outer wooden perimeter fences. Such advice though, was ignored and the fencing was further strengthened. Perhaps three serious incidents in little over seven years should have been warning enough of an alarming tragedy which was waiting to present itself.

CHAPTER ONE

COUNTDOWN TO DISASTER

Glasgow awoke on the second day of 1971 with a collective hangover. Celebrations had taken place across the city but partying would now be replaced by excitement and anticipation as supporters braced themselves for the traditional New Year football match between the city's oldest rivals. The morning of 2 January proved to be bitterly cold as the Glasgow winter bit as only a Glasgow winter can. Such freezing conditions though have never deterred the city's football fans from attending the passionate encounter which is an Old Firm derby. The ground underfoot was solid where ice had formed as fans walked briskly to take up their positions in an 80,057 all-ticket crowd. The Celtic support as usual, filled the Broomloan Road terraces at the West End of the stadium while the home support occupied the rest of the ground, including the traditional Copland Road east terracing. The playing surface had been covered for a full week, although this had not prevented the sub zero temperatures from penetrating the grass below, so leaving it extremely hard.

After the New Years Day fixtures, Celtic held an eight point lead over their Glasgow rivals, with Rangers having played one game more. It was Aberdeen though, having played 19 games to Celtic's 18, who headed the Scottish League First Division with 34 points as opposed to second placed Celtic's haul of 31. Aberdeen were in a rich vein of form, having won 13 games in succession. In the days when two points were awarded for a win, Celtic's eight point cushion over Rangers appeared an impossible gap for the Ibrox men to close. The title race looked certain to be fought out between Rangers East End rivals and the Dons from Pittodrie. Nevertheless, intense pride and a lengthy rivalry remained at stake. Rangers additionally, had the chance to avenge a two nil defeat, which they had suffered at Parkhead earlier in the season. The day prior to the Old Firm clash, Rangers had omitted five of their regular players from their 3-1 defeat against Falkirk at Brockville. The team which took to the hard Ibrox pitch though, was virtually at full strength. Gerry Neef was brought in to replace the injured Peter McCloy. There had also been injury doubts about

Colin Stein who had stitches inserted into a leg wound, although he successfully completed a fitness test. Celtic fielded a powerful line-up although it was missing Billy McNeill through injury and manager Jock Stein, for tactical reasons, omitted Bobby Murdoch.

Once the game got under way, it became clear that it would be the park rather than the individual skills of the players which would have the greatest bearing on the afternoon's entertainment. Mistakes were plentiful though understandable considering the tricky playing surface. Jimmy Johnstone and Alfie Conn though, performed in sublime fashion on a stage more akin to a skating rink than a football field. Arguably it was Celtic who created the better chances and had more to offer creatively but the home side refused to be outshone. Rangers preferred the more direct route to goal, although the passing of Dave Smith in such difficult conditions was commendable. Ronnie McKinnon, meanwhile, effectively marshalled the back line while John Greig proved the influential captain as ever. Celtic's Jim Brogan played well in the rear guard and first time skipper Tommy Gemmell proved an able deputy in Billy McNeill's absence.

The match, with little time remaining, appeared to be heading for an inevitable goalless draw as supporters thoughts began to turn to homeward journeys. Dramatically, as the game drew to a close, Celtic's Bobby Lennox crashed a 25 yard left-footed shot against the Rangers crossbar which rebounded for the flame haired Jimmy Johnstone to head home. The Celtic fans at the opposite end of the ground erupted as they unexpectedly sensed victory and two precious points in their search for championship glory.

The game though had a late dramatic twist in store when Celtic's Jim Craig conceded a free kick on the Rangers left, barely a minute later. Dave Smith curled the ball into the penalty area, Derek Johnstone got a touch to it and the prolific Colin Stein fired home. Both the Rangers team and its supporters were ecstatic, as a point had been salvaged when defeat had seemed certain. Stein's late equaliser had kept intact Rangers' New Year unbeaten 50-year record against Celtic at Ibrox. Aberdeen, meanwhile, had beaten St Johnstone by a solitary Jim Forrest goal and, in so doing, had taken the Dons four points clear of Celtic at the top of the league table. Strangely, at the end of the Old Firm game, sections of the Rangers support celebrated by singing 'The Northern Lights of Old Aberdeen' which is difficult to imagine now, considering the recent climate of ill feeling between the two clubs.

With the spoils shared, both sets of supporters began to exit the ground in the ever-embracing mist. The crowd had been particularly well behaved and efficiently marshalled by the 330 police who were on duty at the match.

Arrests outside the ground had totalled just 11 in number while a further two supporters had been arrested inside Ibrox for drunken behaviour. Apart from the two goals at the end of the game, the afternoon had been relatively incident free.

THE TEAMS

Rangers		Celtic
Gerry Neef	1.	Evan Williams
Sandy Jardine	2.	Jim Craig
Willie Mathieson	3.	Tommy Gemmell (Capt.)
John Greig (Capt.)	4.	Jim Brogan
Ron McKinnon	5.	George Connelly
Colin Jackson	6.	Davie Hay
Willie Henderson	7.	Jimmy Johnstone
Alfie Conn	8.	Harry Hood
Derek Johnstone	9.	Willie Wallace
Dave Smith	10.	Tommy Callaghan
Colin Stein	11.	Bobby Lennox
Sub: Alex McDonald (for Henderson)		Sub: Lou Macari (not used)

Referee
W Anderson (East Kilbride)

Linesmen
W McFarlane (Bonnybridge)
WH Quinn (Stewarton)

CHAPTER TWO

THE FINAL WHISTLE

When referee Willie Anderson sounded his whistle to signal the end of the second Old Firm match he had officiated, the bulk of the all-ticket crowd began to shuffle its way up the terraces to reach the exit staircases. It had been a bitterly cold afternoon; fingers, feet and faces were numb from the penetrating elements. Celtic fans no doubt left Ibrox Stadium that January afternoon with feelings of extreme disappointment. They had witnessed victory, only for it to be snatched away in the dying seconds of the game by a Rangers spirit, which had proved as hard as the playing surface. It was Rangers supporters who felt an internal warmth, knowing that the Parkhead foe had failed to gain the upper hand. Rangers half century unbeaten record in the traditional New Year Ibrox fixture too, had been salvaged. Journeys by car, bus, train, underground and foot beckoned as the dark wintry Glasgow sky became engulfed in the increasingly thickening mist. The lure of pubs and homes became the priority where theory and sentiment could be exchanged about the football stalemate which had been witnessed. Drink and food would inevitably provide a solid foundation for analysis and opinion.

The throng of Celtic support primarily headed for the main exit (Stairway 1) at the south west corner of the ground at the junction of Edmiston Drive and Broomloan Road. A smaller exit (Stairway 7) was also available for the use of the Celtic support at the west end of the ground although this in turn, took them around behind the west terracing and out the same gate as those who used exit Stairway 1.

Rangers supporters had the choice of two exit staircases at the East End, which were virtually identical in design. The choice of staircase however, was fundamentally dictated by the individual proximity to it. Stairway 19 was located in the south east corner, bisecting the junction of Edmiston Drive and Copland Road. 'Sister' Stairway 13 was established at the north east corner of the ground with access to Cairnlea Drive and the dogleg, via Harrison Drive, into Copland Road behind. The staircase had the sinister figure 13 displayed on a large white board supported by a pair of towering poles. It had proved to be the quickest and most popular exit to the

Copland Road underground station. The low-level transport had proved the effective and favoured means of travel since the closure of Ibrox railway station in 1962. Thousands of fans would also use the exit to reach nearby Carmichael Street, Brand Street and environs, where supporters' buses would park. Stairway 13's five flights of steps had long proved convenient for Rangers supporters. Between a quarter and one third of those attending Ibrox chose it as their preferred route from the stadium.

After tentatively finding their way up the vast Copland Road terracing – a journey that was often likely to take several minutes – the Rangers support had to negotiate the 80 steep, downward steps which had a rise of 46 feet in 106 feet. The 'option' of which of the seven lanes to walk down though was not one of absolute choice when surrounded by a mass of fellow supporters all eager to reach street level. The descent of almost 100 stairs, broken by four landings, involved forfeiting the right to control one's own movement. The steel handrails were useful as guides but movement was inevitably perpetual. It was common for feet not to touch the ground on what could often be a hair raising passage to the security of Cairnlea Drive below.

The flow of spectators down that steep Stairway two days into 1971 was no different to any other matchday. The mass of people leaving the stadium at exit 13 was, as usual, tightly bunched. Such resulting discomfort was not a unique experience. Between five and seven minutes had elapsed since referee Willie Anderson had sounded his final whistle. Tragedy began to unfold on Stairway 13. An intolerable crush developed. On the right hand side, between the first and second landings, people toppled and fell. Pressure was so intense that sections of the steel handrails twisted, buckled and flattened. It was horror of the most appalling magnitude as body fell upon body. The wooden perimeter fence stood resolute in its concrete moorings preventing any chance of escape. The boundary would not be breached although several people, through a combination of luck, strength and willpower managed to scale the seven feet high obstacle. Such individuals pulled frantically to safety those that they could, over the pointed fencing. Others were not so lucky. Many had their breath sucked out of them and died as they stood. It was a scene of sheer terror, utter desperation and a tragic loss of life in the most horrific of circumstances.

Chief Superintendent Angus McDonald, on duty at the match, was alerted to an incident at exit 13. Upon his instruction, a police contingent made its way to the top of Stairway 13, whereupon a physical cordon was formed both above and below where the accident had happened. Exiting spectators were hastily diverted away from the area, which helped to relieve pressure. Rescue attempts became frantic as efforts were made to pull those who were trapped, clear of the mayhem. Police, supporters and emergency workers combined to remove the dead, dying and injured. It was a hideously graphic scene and those who witnessed it would never forget what they had seen.

Detective Superintendent Joe Beattie, who had been a spectator at Ibrox on the day, took charge of operations as realisation dawned regarding the magnitude of the unfolding incident. Beattie had led the unsuccessful hunt for the infamous serial killer, 'Bible John' in Glasgow during the late 1960s. It became evident, however, that he was now faced with death on a much larger scale. The accident emergency procedure, which was mounted in the wake of the tragedy, was the largest Glasgow had ever seen. Hospitals in the city were put on standby, special telephone lines were installed and a mobile police office set up. 'Operation Emergency' involved some 200 police officers, seven fire engines and 20 ambulances, which operated a shuttle service to the Victoria and Southern General hospitals. Every available member of the St Andrews Ambulance Service staff in Glasgow was called to assist, even those who were off duty.

The emergency services worked to the maximum of their collective ability to help those who had been trapped. Resuscitation techniques were applied to those who lay unconscious and medical assistance was administered to the injured. Others though, were not so fortunate. Bodies were laid out in a neat line on the playing surface from the north east corner flag to the goalpost, whilst others were placed on the indoor running track. Poignantly, jackets were placed over bodies in a makeshift fashion. Rangers manager, Willie Waddell, his assistant, Willie Thornton and Celtic manager, Jock Stein helped to direct stretcher-bearers to the players' dressing rooms which had been hurriedly converted into casualty stations. Staff from Rangers and Celtic united in a common goal to help those who had unwittingly been trapped on Stairway 13.

Incredibly, many spectators who attended the game that afternoon departed from it unaware of the turmoil which they had left behind. BBC's 'Grandstand' programme was nearing completion when Frank Bough, the programme anchorman, announced sketchy details of an incident at Ibrox. Grainy images, vague reports and considerable hearsay brought home to Glaswegians the magnitude of what had occurred prior to 5.00pm at Ibrox Stadium. The afternoon's events in Govan became the unrivalled talking point in pubs across the country. Relatives and friends waited anxiously for the return home of loved ones, powerless to do anything other than hope. Many were reunited with huge relief while others were not so fortunate. Sixty-five supporters perished on that cold afternoon and a further 145 others were injured.

CHAPTER THREE

THE VIEW FROM THE FOURTH ESTATE

John Burrowes was the then News Editor of the 'Sunday Mail' and had just returned to Glasgow after covering the war in Vietnam the previous week

The pace of the game belied the condition of the ground. Had it not been the 'Big Game', some referees would have declared the pitch unfit for play and not even blown the first whistle. But this was Rangers and Celtic. And it was their New Year Game … there was no cancelling that kind of game lightly. The players themselves would have been much more cautious too, had it been another game, for a fall on that ground and skin would be removed, or worse still, a bone could be shattered, marking the end of a career for a footballer. They played with a rare bravery. As any supporter could have told you, Celtic hadn't won a Ne'erday match at Ibrox for half a century and they were out to break that bad record. And why not? Hadn't they beaten the best in the world in recent years, their daring, non-stop offensive play having made them the first British holders of the European Cup?

Celtic showed right from the start that they had the edge in skill and team-work, little Jimmy Johnstone, their brilliant, red-haired winger, again excelling himself and showing a football artistry that was more associated with a fine summer's turf than this stone-hard pitch. But, as always, if Rangers couldn't match the skill, they could meet it with effort and every Light Blue played his utmost, attacking in hectic raids which had the Celtic men gasping. The Rangers regular goalkeeper, Peter McCloy, was on the injured list and, minus this vital star, they had selected their replacement, Gerhard Neef. The big German was naturally out to impress and he was doing that well, diving at full stretch to catch balls and then thundering down on the concrete-hard mud patch in front of goal.

Midway through the second half, the Rangers fans started singing 'The Northern Lights of Old Aberdeen', the anthem of that city … and its football team. The bush telegraph, via some transistor radios they carried, had brought the news that Aberdeen, also playing that day, had scored a goal against St Johnstone and with there being no scoring between Rangers and Celtic that technically made them the League leaders. And the only good news to a Rangers fan if his team wasn't at the top of the League was that Celtic weren't at number one. Thousands lustily sang the Aberdeen song ... and the Celtic fans got the message.

There's no crowd more silent anywhere than Rangers and Celtic fans when the other side scores. It's an uncanny silence; a silence of shame; a noiselessness of disgrace; an eerie and traumatic quiet as they glower at the triumphant colours hoisted and flaunted among 30,000 upraised, outstretched arms 130 yards away at the other end of the park, each man in his own personal ecstasy of his team's achievement.

Neither side scored in the first half and, with only minutes left in the second half, it was still a scoreless draw. Fans were filtering away from the park disappointed they hadn't seen their side score but consoled, at least, that they hadn't been beaten.

Then, in the 89th and last scheduled minute of the game, Celtic's Bobby Lennox, one of the heroes of the European Cup victory, penetrated the centre field from the left wing, and let loose with all his power a left-foot artillery shot from 25 yards. Neef couldn't have stopped it had it not smashed into the goal crossbar. But it trajectoried back onto the field just ten yards from goal where the everywhere man, Jimmy Johnstone, unmarked, was perfectly positioned. His head met the ball and when Neef got his eyes on it, all he could see was a blur and a wild bounce. There it was billowing up the back of the net. It was too much for thousands of Rangers fans in the Main Stand, in the covered enclosure opposite and in the big covered terrace which they called 'The Rangers End'. They couldn't bear to hear that final whistle or the victory cheers at the opposite slope. And the silence among the Rangers fans was a special one. For this was the Ne'erday Game and to start the year with a goal down to Celtic was the worst ever way. It was like having a death in the family. There could be no chance now of them equalising, let alone winning. The final whistle was only moments away. Who could score a goal in such a brief time, particularly when they had already played for 89 minutes without achieving that great moment? Thousands of them turned their backs and started leaving the ground.

For most of the 46,000 at the 'Rangers End' who made that first move to leave, the direction in which they headed was the north east corner of the ground. They could get there by two wide summit corridors which fed fans in at one end from the covered enclosure and from the other end, the covered terrace. They could also go directly up passageways which led to a shorter parallel summit corridor and which, in turn, fed them to a point where all the corridor traffic met. That point was at the head of the big stairway which led down to Cairnlea Drive, the exit used by more fans than any of the others because of its handiness to the nearby Underground station in Copland Road and to the streets in the vacinity used for parking by the scores of supporters' buses.

The big Stairway was divided into seven passageways by six rows of tubular steel railings. It went down from the top of the terrace to the bottom in 80 steps, broken by four landings, the first after 11 steps, the others after three rows of 17, and then finally 18 steps down to the big concourse in front of the exit gates to Cairnlea Drive. The Stairway was 106 feet long and went down a total of 40 feet at an average gradient of 25 degrees. It was Stairway 13.

The Celtic players were jumping about in their triumph like a circus acrobatic troupe who had just run onto the sawdust. They jumped on little Johnstone, the weight of them burying his red hair from sight as he bent forward under the onslaught of their celebration antics. Then they turned and ran over together to do the same for Bobby Lennox whose magnificent shot which had so narrowly missed had been the creation of the goal.

The Rangers players had no time for commiserations … they were all sprinting madly for the centre of the field, one of them almost losing his balance on the surface of the pitch, now totally in the grip of the new night's hard frost, accompanied by a thickening fog slowly swirling along the track edge. They screamed at each other to get into place quickly so that whatever seconds were left could be utilised for the goal possibility that had eluded them for 89 and a half minutes.

The Rangers forwards gave the ball a long boot as soon as the restart whistle went and the whole team cavalry-charged to the Celtic end in a desperate final attack; an athletic frenzy, the like of which exhausted marathon men can miraculously produce in the final yards of their 26 miles. It was a total risk, total effort, total commitment, the like of which can only be created in such moments, and they were blatantly defying the frightening condition of the iced ground with the speed and verve of their play. Jim Craig, the Celtic defence man was whistled for an infringement. The referee stood erect, his left hand, fist clenched, held high in the air, the sign for an indirect, or non-scoring free kick. Rangers Dave Smith quickly placed the ball on the frozen turf and with the quickest of assessments about where he should punt, thudded it across goal with all the precision he could muster in the direction of some of the high headers, like Derek

Johnstone, the strapping young teenager with renowned heading ability. Had he not won the Scottish League Cup final for them against this very same Celtic just months previously?

The spinning black-and-white ball floated over to the Celtic penalty box and a group of players rose together. But Johnstone's was the head that connected. The ball changed course in a downward ricochet to be met by another scramble of boot-flying players right in front of the goalmouth. One boot got to it ... the man whom they had sang earlier was their Eusebio: Colin Stein, the £100,000 man, the costliest-ever signing in Scottish football. And that single boot to the ball which only the net stopped was worth every penny to the Rangers' fans, halted to a man in their exit scurry to witness the miracle of Ibrox.

Up in the main stand they were jumping on to the wooden seats and benches and stomping on the wooden floor so that it rumbled like a thunderclap. In the elite Members' Section of that stand – the quintessence of Rangersism, dotted with expensive tailored sheepskins and camel hairs, where the language and sentiments could be as vile as the worst sections of the terracing – the elation was unbounded. Dunkirk had become El Alamein in the space of seconds; they hadn't won, but the fact they hadn't lost to Celtic on their own ground was as good as a victory.

The huge cheer brush-fired up the terracing, along the corridors and passageways crowded with exiting fans, and down the exit stairs and out onto the wide concourse and into the streets around Ibrox, now swarming with the thousands who had missed one of the most historic goals in the long history of the Club. No one heard the long piercing sound that came from the referee's lips as he put his round chrome whistle to his mouth to signal the game had run its full course. It was all over. Not even the players heard it for they were all descending on Johnstone and Stein to jump and dance in the triumph. It had been the Celtic men's turn this time to scramble back to the centre in case the miracle could be repeated, but they were only half-way there when they saw the referee run to pick up the ball and head with his linesmen for the tunnel.

It was about 5.15 when I heard the first call on the police radio as I sat at the News Desk, still on my own, the two journalist production executives fast filling up the paper which would run throughout the night with as few changes as possible.

"... bleep ... escort for ambulance at Ibrox Park ..." The message was repeated twice, followed by a variety of other calls, accidents, housebreakings, fights and other miscellany. Then there was a second call, this time for other units to attend at Ibrox where, a voice said, they were getting reports of some kind of incident, the details of which they didn't know, but that one spectator was dead and several had been injured. Without waiting for further details, I ordered a car and was on my way to Ibrox.

Rodger Baillie was a journalist with the 'Sunday Mirror' and attended Ibrox Stadium to report on the Rangers versus Celtic match for his newspaper.

The floodlights beamed down on the ghastly scene, piercing the gloom of the freezing fog swirling around Ibrox Park. I looked down from the press box and struggled to take it all in. There in a neat row behind the goal at the Rangers end, were the bodies of the 66 supporters lying on stretchers. If I close my eyes I can still see them. An eerie silence had descended on a ground that, just a few hours earlier, had been bouncing with wild, raucous celebration. Those 66 fans had been among the thousands at the Rangers end cheering wildly along with their pals as Colin Stein's last minute goal wiped out Jimmy Johnstone's opener to earn Rangers a 1-1 draw against Celtic. The vast majority of the 80,000 crowd left the ground on the night of Saturday 2 January 1971 chattering about that dramatic end to the Ne'erday derby. As they made their way towards cars, buses and homes, they were totally unaware that the match they had just watched would be forever etched into a black-bordered episode in football history known as the Ibrox disaster.

It had taken a long time for the Rangers end to clear after the final whistle, as their fans celebrated that goal. Rangers, apart from a League Cup final win against their oldest rivals two months earlier thanks to a winner from 16-year-old Derek Johnstone, had enjoyed little success against Jock Stein's Celtic. A face-saving draw was almost as good as a win. I watched their joy from the press box. In those days at Ibrox it was perched high on the main stand where the Club deck is today. It was built in the style of a mock castle, and, incredibly, the only entry was by a spiral staircase. Had it ever caught fire there would have been another tragedy. Each newspaper had a kiosk at the back of the box from which reporters phoned in their copy, and from there we had an eagle's eye view of the pitch far below.

As I filed my match report to the Sunday paper I then worked for, something made me glance casually downwards. Suddenly my mind dramatically switched from the details of the match report I was dictating as I saw a score of policemen sprint across the pitch to the terracing at the

Copland Road end of the ground, vault over the wall and dash up the steps. My first thought was that crowd trouble had broken out. Supporters' battles were no rarity then, especially at Old Firm games. But, within seconds, more police were running from the players' entrance, followed by ambulancemen. From my vantage point I could see as far as the edge of the rim at the top of the terracing, with a few hundred fans standing as if paralysed, looking down. I didn't know that the ill-fated Stairway 13 leading from the ground had become a tangle of twisted metal and piled-up bodies, an exit which led to the deaths of 66 fans, all by suffocation, and injuries to another 145.

Back on the pitch, I could see the blood-stained faces of fans being treated by dozens of nurses, white-coated doctors, ambulancemen and policemen. I saw one nurse kneeling on the turf to give one man the kiss of life. Around them lay the bodies of victims, some only youngsters, many of them still wearing their Rangers scarves. It was a scene from hell.

Within the bowels of the old ground, the players remained unaware of the tragedy as they showered and changed. Celtic boss Jock Stein told me later that he had taken a phone call from a 'Hoops' fan in the Persian Gulf, and he had then gone for a quick bath! His players had gone and he was alone in the dressing room. Stein said: "I was looking round to check that no one had left anything when a stream of stretchers started flowing into the dressing-room. I couldn't believe it. Only a short time before it had been filled with my players, now it was the injured and the dying. A man gasped to me: 'There are four dead.' His pal snapped at him: 'Don't exaggerate, there are only two.'

Despite the valiant efforts of all the care workers and the Rangers and Celtic staff – Ibrox chiefs Willie Waddell and Jock Wallace and Jock Stein, helped carry stretchers with the victims – the death toll rose dramatically. Yet none of us was prepared for the final tally. All evening there had been rumours about the number killed. Those speculating on a figure as high as 40 were accused by other pressmen of scaremongering. Eventually the journalists were assembled in the Blue Room at the top of the main marble staircase inside Ibrox and when the Chief Constable of Glasgow, Sir James Robertson, read out the figure of 65 dead a gasp of horror went round the gathering. The first victim was named – a 15-year-old boy from Glasgow.

Elsewhere in Scotland, as the news seeped out slowly from Ibrox, fears grew when loved ones had not returned. Alex Ferguson has told how he and his father and a family friend searched Govan for his brother, Martin, who had been at the game. Eventually he turned up, totally unaware like so many more at the match of what had happened. The Old Firm were united in grief. There were memorial services attended by officials and players from both sides at

St Andrews Roman Catholic Cathedral and then Glasgow Cathedral and a game in aid of the disaster fund was staged at Hampden. Rangers manager Willie Waddell took charge of the Club's reaction as the confused, elderly directors of the Club were paralysed by events. The Ibrox club's matches were cancelled for a fortnight. When they resumed against Dundee United there was a two minute silence and fans were handed a free black-bordered programme with the names of the dead. Waddell wrote: "These have been black days at Ibrox, days of anguish and grief. The scar is deep."

One theory put forward instantly on that night as to why the disaster happened grew to become accepted fact. It was claimed that Rangers fans on their way out of the ground heard the roar that greeted Colin Stein's equaliser, tried to get back up the stairs to join the celebrations and collided with those coming down. But it was never proved and, despite an official inquiry, the true reason for the tragedy may never be known. But the best memorial to the dead is the rebuilt Ibrox Stadium whose architect in truth was Waddell. Every time I listen to ludicrous calls to bring back terracings – and former Minister of Sport Kate Hoey made such a plea – I think angrily of the two disasters I have witnessed, Ibrox and Heysel. And thank God that safety standards have improved so much that no family should ever again have to undergo the anguish of those who suffered so much over 36 years ago.

Shane Fenton, a sports correspondent with the 'Glenrothes Gazette', recalls his personal memories of the Ibrox Disaster in which five of his friends died.

The morning of 2 January 1971 was like any other matchday morning for us young Old Firm fans from the south end of Markinch, with the usual mickey-taking, banter and side bets.

Pete Lee, Johnsy Bett, Joe Mitchell and myself, all Celtic fans, walked from Markinch along with Dougie Morrison, Peter Easton, Ron Paton, Mason Phillips and Bryan Todd, all Rangers followers. We were headed for the CISWO Club in Glenrothes where we would board the rival supporters club buses. Despite supporting different teams, we were all the best of mates and most of us played for the then Markinch United football team. Little did we know that, as we boarded our buses, it would be the last time we would see our pals.

The match itself was nothing out of the ordinary and looked to be heading for a no-scoring draw when Celtic scored in the last minute. We decided to leave at this stage and were actually back on our bus for some 15 minutes when some of the older supporters arrived and told us that Rangers had equalised.

At that time, we knew nothing of the tragic events that were happening on Stairway 13. In fact, it wasn't until our bus made a stop in Kincardine on the way home that we heard something had happened at the Rangers end of Ibrox. The older fans who had been at the pub for a refreshment had heard the news on the television. We never thought for a minute that the Markinch boys were involved.

When I got back home, many locals had already started to panic. My relatives, like those of the other boys who knew we were at the match had already started inquiring to make sure we were all okay. When the news eventually came through that Ron, Dougie, Bryan, Peter and Mason hadn't returned with the Rangers bus, all kinds of thoughts went through our heads. We hoped that they had just missed the bus and would arrive home later. We stayed out until late evening hoping they would appear off the last buses and trains into Markinch.

It was over the next couple of days when the devastating news that we feared had become a reality. The whole village was in total shock with the news that our five friends had been victims of the terrible disaster. The next few days, Markinch, particularly Park View – the street where four of the boys lived – was awash with reporters, photographers and television news crews.

When it was time for the funerals, almost the entire town of Markinch, then population 2,344 turned out to mourn the five local schoolboys. Three of the boys were buried side by side at Markinch Cemetery. The services for the other two were held at Kirkcaldy Crematorium. I can remember the cortege stretching back along the streets lined with mourners. Rangers chairman, John Lawrence, attended the service at Markinch along with half a dozen players.

The boys may be gone, but 36 years on they are still remembered by the people of Markinch. Their names come up periodically when we recall schoolboy tales in our pub conversations. There is a permanent reminder to us all with the memorial plaque, which is situated at the end of Park View.

The tragedy affected many people in different ways. For me, it put me off attending many more senior football matches. Before the disaster, I could count on one hand the amount of Celtic matches I had missed in the previous four years. Since it, I probably wouldn't need one hand to count the games I've been to.

Peter Semple, was a sub-editor with the 'Sunday Mail' who arrived for work with two colleagues only to discover a strike had been called so they were unable to do their shifts. Fate took them to Ibrox.

We went for a few drinks and then somebody came up with the idea of going to the Old Firm game. However, when we got there we were very late and the gates were closed. But they let us in about 20 minutes into the second half.

When Rangers equalised near the end, we waited ten minutes before deciding to make our way towards the exit at Stairway 13. It was a bit of a crush as we approached the top of the stairs and I was trying and succeeded in getting away from the perimeter fencing into the middle, which turned out to be a bad idea. As we went down I was curling my toes trying to keep on my slip-on shoes but I soon gave up. Then I realised we had come to a complete stop. The pressure of the crowd felt like a giant vice. I suddenly realised I was standing on someone but couldn't do a thing about it. We were locked in by the crowd. I remember despairing about the person underneath and how he could not possibly get out. It was horrible.

People were shouting to us all to move back but we couldn't move anywhere. After a while I felt my own life draining away. I had accepted I couldn't last much longer. But for some reason, I decided to try to reach the fencing to my right. I don't know where I got the strength from but somehow I managed to get a hold of the fence and pull until I got out of the vice. I grabbed one of my pals and then saw the other further down the Stairway. We managed to get him out too.

I remember the ten or 11 dead bodies when the police managed to clear the Stairway and the poignancy of hundreds of shoes lying on the steps. Incredibly, I saw my own and a policeman threw them to me but I never went back to an Old Firm game.

Randolph Caughie was a 22 year old news photographer working for the 'Sunday People'. Thirty-six years on his memories remain undiminished.

It was with some reluctance that I attended the Old Firm game at Ibrox. I was on a real high as my daughter had been born the day before. However,

I had a job to do and photographic coverage of the big match had to be done so I headed off to Ibrox by car. I took up my position along the side of the goal with about two dozen other photographers at the traditional Celtic end of the stadium. It was from this location that I recorded the match action as it unfolded.

The end of the game proved to be the most dramatic part as firstly Celtic scored and then Rangers equalised with virtually the last kick of the game. I managed to get a picture of Colin Stein's late goal and at the final whistle headed briskly to my car to drive to the paper's office in Bothwell Street.

Upon my return, my films were handed to a printer ready for developing and then wiring to the paper's office in London. I remember a knock at the office door at 5.10pm and a journalist informed me that there had been some kind of disturbance at Ibrox. I collected my photographic equipment together and headed back to the stadium in my car. I recall that it was difficult to fight my way through the massive crowds that were still leaving Ibrox. I arrived at 5.25pm and managed to gain access to the stadium through the huge blue gates in the south west corner of the ground. I spoke briefly to an ambulanceman who told me that there were several casualties at the other end of the ground.

I remember how eerie the atmosphere was as I raced across the park. My abiding memory though is the silence. Only half the floodlights were on and it was both foggy and cold. The first two people I saw were Willie Waddell and Jock Stein who were carrying a stretcher and this proved the first of many dramatic pictures I took during that early evening. Bodies were brought down from the terrace and laid along the touchline at the side of the goal, which made for a harrowing sight. I can vividly recall an ambulanceman going along the line and holding a small mirror to the mouth of each body and declaring each in turn as being dead.

I left Ibrox at 5.45pm to drive back to Bothwell Street, a journey that took me only ten minutes. I again handed my film to the printer who took it away for developing before it was wired to London, a process that took less than ten minutes. During this procedure, I had spoken to the editor of the *Sunday People* in London who asked about the dramatic events at Ibrox. I know it is a cliched expression but I literally told him to "hold the front page".

On 2 January 1971, I experienced a complete contrast in emotions. It began with the elation of the birth of my daughter and ended in the terrible witnessing of so many deaths. Even after all these years, I can still remember the detail as if it was only yesterday.

Roddy Forsyth, journalist and broadcaster, was 17 years old when he attended the ill-fated Old Firm game.

In 1971, I attended Allan Glen's School – long since abolished, unfortunately – in the centre of Glasgow, along with boys from all over the city and beyond. The school was notable for quite a social mix, from scholarship boys whose backgrounds were often very restricted financially to lads from wealthy households; it also accommodated support for all the Glasgow football teams of the time.

Unlike St Mungo's Academy, a couple of hundred yards along Cathedral Street, which was very much a Celtic stronghold with a smattering of Clyde fans, Allan Glen's had a large number of followers of both Old Firm clubs as well as fans of Partick Thistle, Clyde and Queen's Park. I had friends who liked to go to watch more than one team but I couldn't find anyone to go with me to see Partick Thistle play Stirling Albion at Firhill on New Year's Day.

Even my pals who were Jags devotees were unenthusiastic about going to the game, which was a surprise because Thistle were well into a run of good form that would see them win promotion with most of the players who would take part in the legendary League Cup final victory over Celtic at Hampden later in the same year. The absent friends missed Bobby Lawrie scoring both goals in a 2-0 win that kept Thistle's momentum going at the top of the table.

Now that players and managers commonly complain about fixture congestion and pine for a winter shutdown, it is odd to remember that in Scotland at New Year it was common for teams to play on consecutive days. While Thistle were beating Stirling Albion on Ne'erday, Rangers lost 3-1 to Falkirk at Brockville. That result raised eyebrows but it was not the shock it would be considered now because Rangers had been in fairly dismal form – St Johnstone and Ayr United beat them before Christmas – and by the time of the New Year derby at Ibrox they were well off the pace; 11 points behind Aberdeen – who were Celtic's only challengers – if memory serves. So it was disappointing but not unexpected when I couldn't find anyone to go with me to Ibrox for the 2 January fixture.

A couple of Celtic-minded boys in my class said they would come but in the end they didn't bother to buy tickets and the Rangers crew were flatly disinterested in going to watch what they were sure would be a sound beating by Jock Stein's side. Old Firm games, especially when there were only two league meetings a season, usually sparked a ticket frenzy but on his occasion I remember that there were only a few people about on the day I nipped along to Ibrox to book my place in the crowd.

I went to Ibrox by subway and was most surprised when I got on at Buchanan Street to find John Greig sitting opposite me. The lack of passion amongst both sets of fans, the slow sale of tickets, the captain of Rangers travelling to the ground on a training day by public transport, Rangers losing to Falkirk on Ne'erday – with hindsight it seems that everything combined to deprive this particular Old Firm occasion of passion. And that was how the game felt, too. January 2 was one of those flat, calm days – when the mist never really lifts – which are not unusual in Scotland around the turn of the year. At Ibrox, Parkhead and Hampden at that time the slope of the grounds from end to end was long and fairly shallow, so that if you stood at the top of the terracings behind either goal at an Old Firm game you could watch a spectacle that disappeared with the advent of more compact all-seated grounds.

In those days, if an Old Firm derby goal was scored by the team whose support was massed at the other end of the ground there was a discernible gap between the sight of the celebrations at the far end and the sound of them. The effect was to witness a huge flat mass of distant people become a crazy seething mob in utter silence – the impact of the goal on the other fans was to create a total vacuum of sound – and then half a second later to hear the noise arrive like a tidal wave cascading across a beach. The contrast was always heightened by the fact that the fans of the team that had conceded the goal would fall completely silent for a few seconds before they came bellowing back with their own songs to blank out the racket from the other side. And, of course, in the days of terracings, the mix of supports was not far off half and half.

Sean Connery told me many years later that his sons had been quite amazed by what they saw the first time they attended an Old Firm derby. "I took my two boys to a Rangers-Celtic match and they'd never seen anything like it in their lives. The atmosphere was electrifying and they couldn't believe that when a goal was scored, one end of the park would go demented, dancing and singing, while the other end of the park was absolutely, utterly silent." That sense of excitement is very important in football. However, there was very little excitement about the 1971 New Year derby at Ibrox and the mist meant that the fans at each end of the ground were almost veiled from each other. I can hardly remember anything about the game itself except for the Rangers fans singing 'The Northern Lights' by way of supporting Aberdeen's challenge, which was a pretty forlorn attitude to bring into an Old Firm game.

One thing I do recollect very clearly is the young man and his girlfriend who were standing next to me. At half time they brought out a bag with sandwiches and fruit and gave me an apple. A few minutes from the end, with the game looking as though it would drift towards a goalless draw, they said goodbye and headed off towards the Copland Road end of the ground. I have often wondered if they were caught up in what followed.

Everybody knows that Jimmy Johnstone scored for Celtic in the last minute and that almost straight from the restart, Colin Stein equalised for Rangers. The final whistle blew just a few seconds after Stein's goal. The Celtic fans who had been celebrating what they thought was a win started to head for home right away but you could see Rangers fans spilling back down the terracings to celebrate, while others were trying to make their way up towards the exits. There was quite a bit of confusion and jostling.

I used to wait inside the ground for a fair while at the end of Old Firm games in order to avoid the crushes on the stairs. At Celtic Park, some of the Stairways were narrow and you could feel crushed quite easily. At Ibrox, the problem was that the exit stairs were very steep and there were always people who took them on the run and didn't care who got in the way.

I used to take the subway back across the river and again, because of the jostling and crushing on the platforms of the old Copland Road station after a game, I found it was better to walk along Paisley Road West to Cessnock or even Kinning Park and let the crowding subside. At this game I waited and walked round to Stairway 19, which was best placed for Paisley Road West and I actually passed along the top of Stairway 13 a few minutes after the end of the game. By that time, the disaster had actually taken place but I clearly remember a policeman at the top of the terracing chatting to fans as they passed. He had a grey plastic walkie-talkie unit clipped to his tunic breast pocket and yet he appeared not to know anything about what was going on only about 20 or 30 feet away.

In fact, I left the stadium without seeing or hearing anything wrong and I was quite a distance along Paisley Road West before I heard the first ambulance sirens, which I took to mean that there was probably a fight going on. I took the subway to Kelvinbridge and went to my youth club to play snooker. At about half past six, somebody came in with an *Evening Times* which I think had a headline saying that six people had died in an accident at Ibrox. It was only at about 8.00pm, by which time there were reports of 30 or 40 people dead that I thought I should phone my parents who were, of course, very worried indeed. Even then, we still had no real idea of just how bad this tragedy had been.

Allan Herron, at that time, chief sportswriter at the 'Sunday Mail', recalls his encounter with his friend, Willie Waddell.

It must have been four or five days after the horror of Stairway 13 that I decided to drop in at Ibrox to see how the Rangers manager, Willie Waddell, was coping with the grim consequences of the 1971 catastrophe. It is well documented that 66 people died and 145 were injured as they tried to leave the ground after the 1-1 draw with Celtic. As I entered the manager's office at the top of the marble stairs, I found myself facing another victim – Willie Waddell. I was shocked by his appearance. He looked worn out. A cigarette in his hand, an ashtray on overspill. How much sleep had he had?

I had known Willie as a colleague during my years on the sports desk of the *Evening Citizen* in Glasgow in the early 1950s while he was still a Rangers and Scotland player. We lunched together most days. When I visited Willie back in 1971, it was as a friend, though I was then chief sportswriter of the *Sunday Mail*. I wasn't taking notes!

It did not surprise me that Willie had taken the responsibility of making contact with the injured and the relatives of those who had died on that January match day. Additionally, he made sure that a representative of Rangers Football Club would attend every funeral, be he player, director, member of the coaching staff or management staff which included himself. At that time, Willie ran Rangers just as the manager who had signed him on a £2-a-week contract in 1938 had done – Bill Struth, a strict disciplinarian with a zero tolerance mentality. A fair bit of Struth had rubbed off on Willie.

I am convinced to this day that Willie Waddell's life changed following the tragic circumstances of that infamous Stairway. I was at Ibrox that day but the full impact of the horror was hidden from me by the steep terracing steps though I was aware that people had been injured. It was only after I had left the ground that I learned of the loss of human life.

Though Waddell, then aged 49, was to take Rangers to their greatest ever success the following year when they beat Moscow Dynamo 3-2 in the final of the European Cup Winners Cup in Barcelona, I knew that he had been scarred. That day in his office, his desk littered with files, letters, notes and directories, Willie told me one harrowing story after another. The complicated lifestyle of some families, the loss of an only child, the grief of a young wife with a family, those unaware their loved one had gone to see a football match, and so on. As he sifted through what he and Rangers had to and must do, in the best interests of the bereaved families, in particular he knew it would take months before he could satisfy himself that he had done all he could to ease the pain of the families affected. The names of those who had died, carefully listed, remained in his desk throughout his years as manager and general manager. Those minutes of Stairway panic and the fight for survival was the low point in Waddell's career. How it affected his family, I can only guess.

When I left Ibrox that January afternoon, the stadium was strangely quiet. There was no one about as I walked passed the giant moose head outside the manager's office and down the marble staircase dominated by the portrait of the legendary Alan Morton on the wall. I let myself out of the front door. I left behind a man alone; Willie Waddell, with his thoughts. His pain.

CHAPTER FOUR

PERSONAL RECOLLECTIONS

Donald S Taylor was 17-years-old and travelled to the game with the Wishaw branch of the Rangers Supporters Club. He watched the game with his friend Ian Thom.

I had been a regular attender at Rangers matches since the start of the 1967/68 season and was familiar with the inherent dangers faced when large crowds congregated at any of the three main stadia in Glasgow. Nevertheless, I accepted the risk like everyone else.

I remember that Ian and I watched the game from the Copland Road end, directly behind the goal and approximately halfway up the terracing.

My abiding memory is the weather – it was a cold, bleak January afternoon with the stadium blanketed in freezing fog. The ground was obviously hard underfoot and the game itself was incident free apart from, as I remember, a somewhat erratic display from the Rangers goalkeeper, Gerry Neef. The first goal was scored at the traditional Rangers end and is vividly remembered as it was scored with a header from the diminutive winger, Jimmy Johnstone. The Stein equaliser was seen in silhouette through the gathering gloom.

The final whistle sounded almost immediately and the teams left the field as large sections of the home support sang 'The Northern Lights of Old Aberdeen'! This would be strange to imagine today, given the animosity that exists between players and supporters of the two clubs now. Aberdeen were top of the league at the time and as Rangers had just denied Celtic a point, this meant the status quo had been maintained. At least five minutes elapsed between the final whistle and Ian and myself making our way directly to the top of Stairway 13. At this point we became separated. The pressure of the crowd at the top of the terracing was as always, intense. At the top of the stairs I was at the front of the crowd and could observe the deserted Stairway – supporters re-entering the Stadium was indeed a myth.

Tubular steel divided the stairs into seven passageways and your route was dictated by the constraining influence of the exiting crowd. The pressure remained severe as I was forced down the middle channel.

Suddenly, between the second and third landings, the weight and intensity eased completely. It was at that point as I later realised, the crowd had collapsed in on itself just over my right shoulder. However, I continued to walk unhindered to the bottom of the stairs where, by chance, I was re-united with Ian. Upon turning round and looking back up the stair it became obvious a major incident had occurred. At this point a policeman appeared at our side and told us to clear the area.

The first official indication of what had taken place, came on the way home on the bus via the radio at approximately 5.15pm.

On arrival back in Wishaw, anxious relations, including my own father met the bus and indeed, relations had come to the house from far and near as the news filtered through. A scene that was repeated no doubt, up and down the land.

On a day in which history in the making was witnessed, it has always perturbed me that false theories still persist. For example, the often repeated fallacy that supporters re-entered the Stadium via Stairway 13 upon hearing Colin Stein's goal. Additionally, I do not believe that anyone would have had either the space or nerve to carry a fellow supporter on his shoulders as supposedly witnessed by a resident of Cairnlea Drive.

I remain convinced that weight and volume of numbers were the main cause of what unfolded that day.

Tom Donaldson, of Wishaw, joined the St Andrews Ambulance Association as a 16-year-old in 1965. He was on duty at Ibrox Stadium.

I remember that I travelled to the game on the Wishaw supporters' bus, as my arranged private transport was unavailable. I was part of a team of four first aiders stationed on the trackside below Stairway 13 at the East End of the stadium. From memory, I recall that around 70 first aiders were on duty that day. Unlike now, we had no means of communication between first aiders on the ground; there was no command and control structure. Our volunteers were neither equipped nor trained in major incident management and our first knowledge of anything untoward was when my colleagues and I were asked to go to the top of passageway 13 where there had been a crushing incident.

When I arrived at the top of the perimeter of the standing area, people were staring down into the stairwell. Spectators with minor injuries were already staggering from the scene and were being comforted by fellow spectators. As I looked down the Stairway, people were moving away from the bottom; some were on the grass verge at the right hand side either uninjured or dazed. Some supporters made their way back to the top of the Stairway to relative safety whilst others just stood as if they were frozen to the spot. At the heart of the incident, all that could be seen was a mass of bodies, which were entangled. By this time it would be almost 5.00pm and darkness was falling.

Spectators with minor cuts, bruises and upper limb fractures were directed away from the scene. Those with lower limb back injuries or those still trapped were stabilised. Many others were treated for asphyxia by mouth to mouth ventilation. Sadly, only those who had resuscitation attempts made in the early stages of the incident had successful outcomes, despite the availability of oxygen. The majority of those who died suffered traumatic asphyxia.

Unlike today there was no Scottish Ambulance presence in the ground. No one had ever heard of a Major Incident Plan or Major Incident Management. There was no organisation at the scene, no forward control, triage officers or casualty clearing stations. Valuable time and resource was used transporting casualties. The walking wounded were escorted to the trackside and from there to the First Aid Room. Further temporary treatment stations were set up on the trackside and a temporary mortuary arranged in the dressing rooms. As ambulance vehicles and personnel arrived, the more serious casualties were loaded onto ambulances either at the trackside or at the Cairnlea Drive exit.

In those days there was no responsibility on the Club or the St Andrews Ambulance Association to provide a doctor for any instances of injury or illness in the crowd. The Club Doctor did, however, assist in the early stages and later there was a response from the Health Board. Unfortunately, by the time this resource was available, the prime function was to certify death, as most of the severely injured but viable patients had already been transported to hospital.

There has been speculation over the years that the cause of the accident was the Rangers support turning back up the stair as the crowd roared in excitement when Rangers equalised. I do not though, hold with such reasoning. Only those at the top of the Stairway would have had any chance of sharing in the celebrations. I am more inclined to believe, for whatever reason, someone slipped on the Stairway and whether by further pressure or imbalance in the crowd flow to avoid the fallen spectator, this set up a cascade and the crowd just tumbled into a falling mass.

My lasting memory of that terrible day was the scale of the disaster and regret that more could not have been done. There was a hopelessness that our resource was so inadequately trained and equipped for the task in hand. I will never forget the scene of the bodies on stretchers, which were neatly laid around the perimeter of the playing field.

Sgt Walter Muir was in charge of the temporary Police Office inside Ibrox Stadium on 2 January 1971 and was assisted by other Enquiry Department Constables.

Having a temporary Police Office is normal practice at football grounds during big matches; this is in addition to the normal police presence for crowd and traffic control. For an 'Old Firm' game there were remarkably few incidents, only two or three arrests where we would normally expect upwards of 50 at this particular New Year fixture.

I remember it was a cold, dry day with a slight mist. The match had just finished when I was informed of an accident at passageway 13. I left the office and went across the ground to the passageway. By then, injured and dead were being laid along the edge of the field. I made my way up the terracing to the top where I saw the fallen supporters in heaps on the stairs. Everyone who could possibly help was pulling out the dead and injured. I joined them in the rescue work until called onto the track where I met the Chief Constable. He instructed me that he had arranged for a Mobile Incident caravan to be situated outside the main entrance of Ibrox Stadium where my enquiry constables could assist people searching for their missing relatives and friends and where telephone engineers were installing lines to cope with the rush of calls. This was where concerned people came for information.

Many traumatic incidents have stuck in my mind since the day of the disaster. An elderly couple came to me enquiring after their son. From their description I was afraid he was one of the bodies I had pulled from the crush. In their distress, they were hoping against hope that 'he could just have been late for the bus' or 'was with friends.' Later that night, the sergeant in charge of the temporary mortuary told me that they had returned and identified their son's body. The poignant sight of so many young boys' bodies and the sacks of shoes gathered from the Stairway, forced from their owners' feet by the terrific pressure, are just some of the memories which remain with me to this day.

Over the following weeks the enquiry continued from Govan Police

Office under the charge of Det. Supt. Joe Beattie; extra police officers had to be brought in from all over the city to cope with the hundreds of interviews and statements.

Incidentally, many theories have been advanced as to the cause of the tragedy. One in particular being brought to my attention later by an elderly lady whose grand-daughter had been on passageway 13. The girl told me that she was being forced down the steps in the crush when an unknown man heaved her up and over the fence onto the embankment. As she was being thrown, she glanced back and saw that the man had fallen under the crowd. This could perhaps explain the figure being carried on someone's shoulders seen by another witness from a window overlooking Stairway 13. The young girl was extremely distressed; she bore the characteristic sign of very bloodshot eyes, which was apparent in all of the victims of the dreadful incident.

The events of that awful day in the history of Ibrox Stadium have remained with me for many years. There was no trauma counselling in those days, it was all 'just part of the job'.

Colin Jackson wore the Rangers number six shirt on that infamous January day in 1971.

I played in the game which resulted in one of the most horrendous accidents ever at a football stadium. Although more than 36 years have passed, it is an event which my memory does not let go of.

I can remember the weather that day being of the typical mid winter type; cold, damp and with a frosty mist. Old Firm games, however, have a unique atmosphere wherever and whenever they are played and this one was certainly no different.

Apart from the usual on and off the ball incidents the game was heading for a goalless draw when, with little time remaining, wee Jimmy Johnstone scored for Celtic. Almost immediately, Colin Stein equalised and I remember the game had hardly restarted again before the final whistle sounded. It was an exciting end to an otherwise hard fought tussle.

Once we were in the dressing room there was a sense of relief that we had not lost the game. Our home record against Celtic was pretty good then. The players headed for the large marble bath which could accommodate 12 players. Initially, there was no indication of there being anything wrong until we heard the odd raised voice. By the time I had dressed half the team had already left. It was about then that the first casualties started to appear on stretchers heading towards the gymnasium which adjoined the dressing room. I can't remember who was with me but we obviously wanted to know what was going on. We looked into the gymnasium to see three or four young lads with their faces a strange colour of blue due to lack of oxygen. At this point we were asked to leave and get off home. Obviously, something had gone seriously wrong and as we left someone said three people had died in an incident. As much as I tried to understand what might have happened I related it to the crazy rivalry that sometimes unfortunately tarnishes the name of two great clubs. How wrong could I be!

Later, as prearranged, I met a couple of mates and we went to Reids Bar in Hope Street in the city centre. They had a television in there and for the first time I realised the extent the accident was becoming. There were people frantically trying to use the pub phone (there were no mobiles in those days) to inform families they were safe. I can clearly remember the death toll being quoted at 46 as reports continued to flood in.

The next few days were spent visiting the injured in hospital. Many still had that blue pallor caused by lack of air. The visiting was followed by the players being given lots of funerals to attend by the Club. This will always live with me as the average age of the young men seemed to be around 24 or 25. It was heartbreaking to listen to the tributes from family members and friends.

I know that there were people better qualified than me to give a fuller account of events from that terrible day. For example, Willie Waddell, Jock Wallace, Physio Tom Craig, Diane Kilgour (the Manager's secretary) and many others worked around the clock to help bereaved relatives. However, my recollection is from a player's angle and I feel the magnificent Ibrox Stadium that stands today is a marvellous tribute to those who died that day.

Jim Craig was Celtic's right fullback on 2 January 1971.

Even for such a momentous match, the details can sometimes be difficult to recall. The record books may show that the second Old Firm encounter of the 1970-71 season ended in a 1-1 draw but what followed afterwards put the importance of football into perspective.

For any player wearing the colours of Celtic or Rangers, these matches can be very demanding. Only the extremely extrovert could fail to be affected by the pre-match tension or the poisonous atmosphere in the ground. Many players are affected so badly by nerves that the final whistle comes as a relief, almost but not quite at the expense of the result.

This match was really important. Celtic only occupied second place in the table, at that time three points behind Aberdeen. Rangers were 11 points adrift of the Dons so they would be desperate for a win to close the gap and hoped that home advantage would make a difference.

When we arrived at Ibrox and walked down the tunnel to inspect the pitch, I must confess that my heart sank. Conditions were poor; just what I really disliked. It had been frosty over the last 24 hours so the ground was quite hard. On top of that, though, the rise in temperature from morning had allowed the surface to melt slightly. The combination could not have been designed for more difficulty, with the choice of studs a debatable one. If I didn't fancy the surface, Bobby Murdoch was even more unhappy and after a chat with Jock Stein, withdrew from the side. Then the team was announced and we took up our respective places in the dressing room to prepare for the match.

To be honest, I have little recollection of the play itself. From what I have read, it seems to have been a typical Old Firm occasion, the physicality of the football more prevalent than the skilful side. With only a minute left, Jimmy Johnstone put Celtic ahead and their fans whistled for the end of the game. In one last charge though, a cross from the left by Davie Smith was bundled in by Colin Stein to salvage a draw.

Afterwards, the Celtic dressing room was not a happy place. Jock Stein did not like losing points at any time; to miss out on the chance of a win over Rangers really annoyed him. Rather quietly, we used the big bath of those days to clean ourselves up and changed back into our street clothes. At that point, there were no internal signs of the problems without.

The door opened and Jock Stein was summoned outside. He came back in again within a few moments to announce that there was some trouble in the Stadium and we were to get on the bus as quickly as possible. We rushed through the crowd in the Ibrox atrium without the chance to speak to anyone and were ushered on to the vehicle parked right beside the front door.

When we heard the word 'trouble' we all assumed that it meant some form of fighting among the spectators, either inside or outside the ground. Once on the bus though, the absence of four people who had travelled with us to Ibrox – Jock Stein, trainer Neil Mochan, physio Bob Rooney and Doctor John Fitzsimons – made some of us wonder just what was going on.

Suddenly, as we pulled away from the ground and headed towards Parkhead, the driver switched on the radio and we heard the tragic news. A reporter informed us that some form of disaster had occurred in a stairway and some people had died. I forget the exact number but as we travelled back to Celtic Park, it continued to rise. Once at the ground, I got into my car, adjusted the radio to the same programme and spent the 20 minutes travelling to my home in north-west Glasgow listening in horror as the death count mounted alarmingly. When I arrived at the house my wife appeared, tears streaming down her face and together we spent the rest of the evening glued to the television set.

My Celtic career encompassed some 231 matches, most of them with happy endings, although I did have the occasional 'bad day at the office'. However, the events of that day, 2 January 1971, put the oft-used football words 'tragedy' and 'disaster' into perspective.

Craig Smith, then aged four, tells the story of his father who perished in the Ibrox Disaster.

My father got up one morning, said his goodbyes, went to a football match and I never saw him again. When you are four years old that is how straightforward your world is. When you get older though, it becomes more of a where? when? and why? My story is as I remember it and from what I have pieced together over the intervening years.

On 2 January 1971, my dad George woke early. It was a big day in Glasgow for football fans as it was the traditional Old Firm New Year derby. I was in the house with my mother, Anne, and my two older brothers, George and Stephen. I remember my dad putting on his coat and scarf to go to the game where he was going to meet his brother, John, brother-in-law Alex and a couple of other people. I asked my dad if I could go with him but he said no as there would be too many people there, although he would take me to the next game. He said goodbye to us all and left. We lived in a multi-storey block of flats at the time and I ran to the kitchen window where I watched him walk down the street. I remember it was bitterly cold and foggy outside as I watched him disappear into the gloom.

My dad met up with the others and they stood in the traditional Rangers end close to Stairway 13. The dramatic end to the game is well documented and upon hearing the final whistle, my dad, John and Alex made there way to the top of the Stairway. At this point they were split up as my dad was forced to the right of the Stairway and John and Alex to the left. The Stadium that day held about 80,000 spectators and I suppose around 13,000 people would have attempted to leave the ground via that Stairway as it led directly to the underground station at Copland Road. I am told that once you had passed over the top of the terracing there was no turning back and you had no control over which section of the Stairway you went down due to the mass of people behind you. I understand it was common to descend the Stairway without your feet touching the ground.

Suddenly there was a blockage on the stairs and the crowd was not moving although people behind continued to surge forward unaware that there wasn't anywhere to go. By now John had passed out due to the sheer weight of people around him. Alex struggled to free himself and watched as John was pulled out of the crush and passed over the wooden fence at the side of the Stairway. People were screaming and crying. Worst of all, people were dying.

At this point my dad was about halfway down the stairs and was crushed between the wooden fence and the people around him. The metal rails between the stairs had given way and he was facing the fence with his eyes open. His lips were blue; he was dead. Alex and John had struggled to move him as he stood upright in a sea of people but their efforts were in vain. My dad was just 40 years old with a wife and three young kids. The man next to him was dead, so was the man in front as were those behind and below. My dad had no broken bones or visible injuries; the life had simply been squeezed from him.

People I have spoken to who were there that day described it as a surreal situation. It was foggy and it was quiet. There was a mass of bodies on the stair; those near the bottom were horizontal and they became more vertical the further up the stairs you went. The victims were taken one by one down onto the pitch behind the goal where ambulance crews and police tried desperately to revive them. For 66 supporters there was no hope. John and Alex left the Stadium that day in a daze, totally shattered and in shock. They walked in silence, with no shoes on, to my grandmother's house.

My gran lived across the road from us and most of the family had gathered there as they were going to a dance later that night at a local golf club. She opened the door to John and Alex. "George is dead" was all that John could say. My gran replied, "That poor lassie and those boys".

Meanwhile, it was a pretty normal day in my house. Christmas presents were being played with and arrangements were being made for my brother George's birthday the following day. The usual Christmas programmes were showing on television when shortly after 5.00pm they were interrupted by a news flash. Sketchy details came through of an incident at Ibrox Stadium in which a few people had been injured. Scottish Television flashed up a picture of Hampden Park, which seemed quite funny at the time. Something though, wasn't quite right and my mum was uneasy as she hadn't heard from my dad and time was passing. He would surely have phoned to say everything was fine. She started phoning various members of the family but no one knew anything. She also phoned the downstairs neighbour who was at the match but at the Celtic end. He didn't know anything about an incident until he got home. Worry was etched on my mother's face.

Then came a knock at the door and Stephen answered it. There stood three of my uncles; Willie, Sam and David. Sam broke the news, "Your dad's dead", and Stephen screamed. A scream I will never forget. My mother came running and I heard Sam say to her, "Anne, George is dead", which was followed by a piercing hysterical scream. In my mind George couldn't be dead because George was my brother and I could see him standing there, kicking and punching the wall. I was four years old and could not work it out. My daddy was my daddy and George was my big brother so who were they talking about? David lifted me up and carried me out of the house to take me over to my gran's. On the way to the lifts he said, "Son, your daddy is dead". I spent the rest of that night and most of the next day still not sure what it all meant.

The rest of the story is how I remember my Uncle Jack relating it to me in later years. He was 33 years of age at the time of the disaster.

My Uncle Jack lived in Govan at the time and had heard the sirens of ambulances and police cars as they passed on their way to Ibrox. On the radio, news came through that some people had been injured at the Rangers ground. Then it was confirmed that two people were dead and 20 were injured before the death toll rose to six. At this point he received a phone call from his brother David, telling him that George had been killed. He remembers thinking to himself that this couldn't be happening. He immediately started out for his mother's house. On the way there he met John and Alex and both of them had no shoes on. They were in total shock with tears running down their faces. He asked them what had happened. 'George is dead, we've lost George', was the most he could get out of them. It was at his mother's house that he made the decision to go to Ibrox to see what he could find out.

As he approached the Stadium, there was a mass of people milling around outside. There were ambulances, police cars, reporters and anxious relatives. He noticed a police caravan outside the main entrance and went inside where he was met by a police sergeant. He explained that his brother-in-law, George Smith had been at the match and was missing. The sergeant directed him through the main entrance of the Stadium. He was taken into one of the player's dressing rooms where he sat down on a wooden bench. There were about 20 other people there all looking worried and frightened. Across from him was a mother and her two daughters. "He'll be alright, maw. He's probably in the house and we're all here waiting for him", said one of the daughters. "If he's in that bloody house, I'll kill him", the mother cried. It dawned on Uncle Jack at that point that these poor people did not know if their loved ones were dead or alive. However, he knew that George was dead. He went up to one of the policemen and said, "Look, I know my brother-in-law is dead". He replied, "Now sir, don't be like that, don't give up hope". He then explained what he already knew and he was taken back outside to the caravan. It was there that they told him to make his way to the city mortuary.

It was a long journey with plenty of time to think and to let it all sink in. He arrived at the mortuary where he was shown into what he described as an auditorium. There must have been around 40 people sitting in there and they were all grim faced. A policeman came to the front and explained what was going to happen. "To make it easier for all concerned", he said, "If you approach this man at the front and try to describe who you are looking for, giving age, etc, then we will do our best to take you to the correct deceased. There are 65 bodies in that other room and we don't want to upset you any more than you have been by having to look at the wrong body". The enormity of the situation then dawned on him. Sixty-five people dead! He thought that there were only six!

He was approached by one of the mortuary attendants and described who he was looking for. He was then taken to another room and on the floor was body after body, all covered with white sheets. There were people leaning over bodies saying, "No, that's not him". People were screaming and crying. He was led to one white sheet and when it was pulled back, there was George. He was lying on his side with his knees up towards his chest. There was not a mark on him except for the bridge of his nose where there was a line running across it as if a wire had been pressing against it. "Yes, that's George Smith," he said and was led from the room. He was taken outside and given a number then told to come back the next day with the number and collect any personal effects.

He spent the next four days with the rest of the family making sure no newspapers arrived at the house and keeping reporters away from the door. On the third of January an envelope was pushed through the door. Inside was £30 and a note which read, 'I am sorry. From a Tim!'

Through years of researching my father's death, I discovered there had been various incidents on that Stairway down the years. In 1969 after another Old Firm game, a crush occurred and people escaped because the wooden fence gave way and allowed an exit route on to the grass verge. After that incident, Rangers Football Club decided to strengthen the wooden fence by replacing it with wooden sleepers embedded in concrete which effectively built a death trap with no means of escape.

There is a website dedicated to the Ibrox Disaster and on it is a short story of mine about my father. Importantly, the names of the 66 supporters who died are also listed. Along with many others, I wrote to Rangers Football Club requesting a permanent tribute to those who had died. I was delighted when the Ibrox Disaster memorial was unveiled on the 30th anniversary of the tragedy.

Donald Montgomery was a Police Officer with the City of Glasgow Police in 1971.

On 2 January 1971, I was on duty at Ibrox Stadium and along with other officers from the Southern Division was detailed for duty on the running track of the Stadium. The procedure at that time was to walk round the track in a clock-wise direction during the first half of the match then in an ante-clockwise direction for the remainder of the match.

At the end of the game I was standing facing the crowd just below passageway 13 when I noticed a spectator waving to us to come to the top of the Stairway. Along with my colleagues I ran to the top of the terracing where I saw a large area had been cleared – always a bad sign – and in the centre of this cleared area what can only be described as a pile of bodies about six feet high and about 15 feet across. It took a few seconds to adjust to this sight. Steam was rising thickly into the freezing air from the pile of bodies. We proceeded to disentangle the bodies and carry the dead and seriously injured back down the terracing on to the pitch where they were laid out in rows. This went on for some time as I recollect and when the last body had been removed, the ground underneath was covered with wallets, shoes, socks, cash, pocket combs and watches which had been forced from the victims by the intense pressure. The steel barriers were twisted like rubber bands.

I then made my way back to the Southern Division HQ at Craigie Street where I remained on duty until 2.00am to assist with phonecalls which were coming in from all over the world. The Govan Division teleprinter was keeping us updated as victims were being identified. Like everyone else who witnessed the tragedy, the trauma remains. I hope that in some small way my actions on that day were of some help, but I will never know.

Andy Ewan was 23-years-old and worked as branch librarian in Alexandria with the then Dunbarton County Council. His friend Mike Taylor had returned home to Aberdeen for the New Year holiday. He attended the game alone.

I was lying face down about four feet from the cold concrete steps, trapped from waist to toe in the massive crush of bodies. It was halfway down Stairway 13 at Ibrox Stadium on 2 January 1971, just before 5.00pm. Immediately around and above me it was strangely silent, with only muffled cries and sobs but higher up, at the top of the Stairway and beyond, I could hear the singing and chanting of happy football supporters. Amazingly, a matter of yards in front of and below my straining body, hundreds of fans were reaching the bottom of the steps and walking casually towards the exit gates, completely unaware of the disaster that they had escaped by seconds.

A policeman, shocked and staring, came up the stairs and began to help those of us at the front of the huge pile of bodies. He was able to pull some people out but I was so tightly jammed that he found it impossible to release me so he moved on. All the time I could feel the tremendous weight on my legs increasing as supporters approaching the Stairway from the passages at the top of the terracing continued to press forward, unaware of what was happening below. There was a sudden movement in the bodies above me, I felt my legs being twisted round and was now left lying almost face up with my back to the ground. Up until then I had felt a sense of shock and unreality rather than fear but now a stab of panic went through me. I could feel the strain on my back increasing and was seriously concerned about what further movement above me might bring. I was lucky – after a few minutes, the crushing weight on my legs seemed to ease slightly and I called to the policeman again for help. This time he gripped me firmly under the armpits and, with a powerful heave, pulled me clear. He half walked, half carried me to the bottom of the Stairway and I collapsed heavily on to the lower steps, still unable to grasp fully what had happened. I had only been trapped for perhaps ten minutes or so but it seemed a lifetime since the referee had blown his whistle for the final time on that fateful afternoon.

Some 20 minutes earlier I had been celebrating Rangers last minute equaliser in a forgettable 1-1 draw with Celtic. Seconds later, as the final whistle sounded, thousands of fans began the frantic scramble to the top of the terracing, heading for the exit stairways. I was 23 at the time and already a veteran of at least a dozen Old Firm matches. Only a few months earlier, I had been among a six-figure crowd at Hampden to witness my team beat Celtic 1-0 in the League Cup final. I was well aware of the crushing that always developed at the exit points after these games, whether at Ibrox, Celtic Park or Hampden and also of the dangers present on the steep terraces during the action.

I waited on the Copland Road terracing for about five minutes before moving towards the exit passageway. I thought that would allow enough time for the initial rush to disperse but I underestimated the numbers still in the ground. In the passageway that ran round the top of the terracing I was quickly aware that, even 20 yards or so away from the top of Stairway 13, a severe crush was developing. I tried to ease myself back to safety but it was already too late to escape from the mass of humanity that was now grinding its way inexorably towards disaster.

Unless you have experienced it, it is difficult to explain just how helpless and vulnerable you feel when trapped in the middle of a large crowd of people, especially on steep or uneven ground. You are completely at the mercy of hundreds of others, many of whom you cannot even see. You are swept along, unable to influence what is happening and can only concentrate on keeping your arms high, out of the crush and staying on your feet. By the time I reached the top of Stairway 13 I was scared. I had been caught up in big match crowds before but never had I experienced the level of pressure that was now being exerted on everyone around me. All of us were suddenly aware that this time it was worse that usual, that danger genuinely threatened. People were shouting, trying to get others to stop pushing forwards from the back and sides but it was hopeless. As we began to descend the stairs I felt a slight tug on the bottom of my jeans and was horrified to just make out the hand of someone on the ground. He was trying desperately but hopelessly to rise against a mass of people so tightly jammed together it was almost unbelievable that he had been able to fall.

Someone else trod on my heel and I immediately pulled my foot out of the shoe, thankful that I was wearing slip-ons instead of my usual lace-ups. My other shoe soon followed as the pressure intensified. People were now really suffering; there were cries for help, agonised gasps for breath and faces with veins and eyes bulging. By this time I was about one third of the way down the stairs and intent only on keeping upright and staying alive.

What happened next? Did a crush barrier buckle under the intense pressure or did people further down the steps simply stumble under the huge weight of the fans above them? I don't suppose we will ever know for sure but suddenly I was falling, amidst flailing, heaving fellow supporters, a mass of us collapsing on to people below and in turn, being buried by those above.

I don't remember how long I sat on the steps, as more police and rescuers began to appear. Eventually I got to my feet and realised that I had lost my supporter's scarf and both shoes and was starting to ache all over. I went back up the stairs and asked a policeman if I could do anything to help. He took one look at me and told me to go home. Cold, bewildered and probably in shock I walked slowly out of the ground. I cannot remember much about the next hour or so but someone in a supporters' bus saw me wandering along the icy pavement in my stockinged feet and took me on board. I tried to explain what had happened, that there were dead and dying people lying on Stairway 13 but I don't think anyone took me seriously. Then, as the bus headed for the city centre, reports started to come through on the fans' radios and the previously cheery atmosphere disappeared. I was dropped off near Bridgeton Cross and eventually got a taxi back to my home in Hillhead. By this time the disaster was the main news item with the death toll rising steadily.

I woke up the following morning feeling sore and exhausted and covered with bruises. Only when I read the Sunday newspapers did I fully grasp the extent of the disaster and realise how lucky I had been. It was undoubtedly the most traumatic event of my life but it did not dilute my love of football or prevent me from continuing to follow Rangers. Two weeks later, I returned to Ibrox for Rangers first match after the disaster and, in May 1971, I attended the Scottish Cup final against Celtic at Hampden amidst a crowd of 120,000. The Ibrox disaster will never be forgotten but the football goes on.

Apart from a brief letter to a national newspaper on the 25th anniversary of the disaster in 1996, this is the first time that I have written down what actually happened to me during the aftermath of the match and I have found it helpful, if also rather traumatic, to relive the experience even after all these years. I am very conscious that I was extremely lucky to walk away from the events of that day and I still think about those poor fans who were less fortunate.

Margaret Lavery (nee Stevenson) was a 28-year-old Nursing Sister at the Southern General Hospital in Glasgow in 1971.

On 2 January 1971, I was on duty at the Accident-Orthopaedic Department of the Southern General Hospital, which was the first purpose-built department of its kind in the United Kingdom. Six nursing staff were on duty that day – myself, two staff nurses, one enrolled nurse and two student nurses. Medical staff on duty were – one Consultant, Mr Whitefield (on call), one senior Medical Assistant (in theatre, operating at 5.00pm), one senior House Officer and one Junior House Officer.

The only method of communication with ambulance, police and fire services was by hospital telephone. There was no independent means of communication. The SGH switchboard had approximately 30 telephone lines. One switchboard operator was on duty on 2 January 1971.

At the end of the BBC's *Grandstand* programme, a brief report of the incident was televised. This, understandably, resulted in the switchboard being flooded by calls from anxious relatives. The switchboard operator must have felt under siege. On seeing the same report, off duty staff of all grades and disciplines rushed to the hospital to help.

At 4.30pm, I returned on duty following a 'split shift' and received a report on the patients within the department from my colleague, Sister J Fowle, who was due to go off duty at 5.00pm. One 33-year-old man with a serious heart condition was causing concern and was being treated by physicians in our resuscitation area.

At approximately 5.00pm, the Head Porter entered the department and informed me that he had overheard an ambulance radio report requesting all ambulances to return to Ibrox as a barrier had gone down. Remembering the 1969 incident at Ibrox, I requested that he brought every available hospital trolley to the department. Simultaneously, I received a telephone call from a police sergeant informing me that a barrier had gone down at Ibrox and to expect approximately 30 casualties. I received no further communication regarding projected amount of casualties. In total between 80-100 patients arrived at the SGH for treatment.

I immediately informed the switchboard operator together with Mr Whitefield and Miss Smith, the Senior Nursing Officer in charge at the SGH, of the incident at Ibrox. My next step was to inform my own staff, reassure the student nurses and, with Sister Fowle, open up all available areas within the department for the reception of casualties. The final step was to clear the department by transferring patients out of the department. The seriously ill heart patient was transferred, safely, to the Coronary Care Unit with physicians in attendance.

At approximately 5.10 – 5.15pm I was approached by two plain-clothes police officers and asked to supply medical assistance to Ibrox. I explained that medical teams should be attending from the second or third hospitals on stand-by. However, I was assured by the police officers that no medical help was, as yet, present at Ibrox and they stated that people were dying in front of their eyes. In the absence of any other means of information or communication and with the SGH and Ibrox football stadium in close proximity to each other, we agreed that Sister Fowle would take the portable emergency equipment and go with the police to Ibrox. I felt so alone at this point.

The dead arrived first and, as the ambulances had to return to Ibrox, we placed the dead on to trolleys within the teaching area of our department. I felt guilty at having to leave them alone. A bus arrived with walking wounded. As they were directed to one area within the department, a never-ending stream of ambulances started to arrive with the more seriously injured fans, at the ambulance entrance to the department. The noise from ambulance sirens, the casualties cries of pain and confusion, which was caused by the lack of oxygen, was deafening.

About this time, Miss Smith arrived in the department and, as it was obvious that the figure of 30 casualties was being greatly exceeded, she ran to the Nurses Home and asked all off-duty nurses to return to their wards – which they all did.

The emergency treatment carried out in the department was mainly oxygenation and cannulation to gain intravenous access for the administration of drugs and splintage of broken limbs.

Mr Whitefield must have arrived within 20 minutes of my telephone call; those minutes were the longest of my life.

The consultants and medical staff carried out cursory examinations within the accident department, followed by secondary examinations when patients were transferred to wards. Some patients were returned to the department for further X-rays and treatment. Once this shuttle system was put into operation, organisation and control was established. Mr Bingham, one of our consultants, organised the transfer of the dead fans to the adjacent rehabilitation building to await identification by loved ones. Consultants in the newly opened Institute of Neurological Sciences made intensive care beds available and two patients were transferred for intensive care treatment. Leverndale Hospital sent nurses in taxis to help.

Dr Bryden, the Deputy Medical Superintendent, worked throughout the night collating the names and numbers of injured with the relevant wards to which they had been admitted. This was an important task, as many of the injured fans had no means of identification on their person.

At one point I turned a corner to find a young policeman standing with a bag of shoes. Inexplicably, my legs became shaky and weak and I had to sit down for a few seconds. I think the sight of the shoes brought home to me the full scale of the tragedy and I was filled with profound sorrow, not only for the individual fans lying dead within our department but for all the other individual fans lying dead outwith the department. Shoes are such individual items of clothing.

The SGH opened its doors for normal business at 9.00pm. I returned home at about 11.00pm to an anxious family who, because they were entertaining visitors, were unaware of the tragedy. It was a difficult journey home because of the fog and my head was spinning with the night's events. Needless to say, I did not sleep. I returned to duty at 7.30am on Sunday morning.

The following days were difficult for ward and orthopaedic staff. Tired and emotionally drained and without any additional staff, we had to cope with our normal workload, plus the extra work engendered by the disaster. Some of my patients required orthopaedic surgery and were in hospital for weeks. No counselling was available for the bereaved, injured or hospital staff.

I have no doubt that the lack of knowledge and understanding of the mechanism of crowd control; the steep incline of Stairway 13 and the catalyst of possibly a stumble, were the significant factors in causing the tragedy.

George Whitefield was the duty consultant at the Southern General Hospital on 2 January 1971.

On the day of the disaster I was working at home and tea was being prepared when the telephone rang. It was Hugh Cuthbert, my registrar. He said he had received a call from Ibrox to say that they wanted a doctor at the stadium and he asked how he should respond. I told him to go immediately and that I would come in and take charge until the situation was clarified. I told my wife that I was going immediately not knowing at that time the extent of the problem. A fast drive without any hold ups took me to the junction of Govan Road and Copland Road from which streams of traffic were emerging. Fortunately, a fire engine came out of Copland Road and I managed to nip in behind it and had a quick run to the Southern General Hospital just as the first emergencies were being brought in.

The SGH sits on the south side of the river Clyde, less than two miles from Ibrox Stadium with the Victoria Infirmary a further three miles south; both received casualties. The Accident and Emergency department at the SGH was the first purpose built A&E unit since the beginning of the NHS and was designed to a pattern proposed by my senior colleague Bill Sillar and myself. Happily, its layout effectively suited the needs of the situation in allowing the easy separation of the seriously injured from the 'walking wounded'. I immediately took over the delegation of duties to the staff available and the designation of areas of treatment for the major and minor injuries.

Due to the BBC 'Grandstand' coverage of the incident at Ibrox, staff began to appear spontaneously and this helped greatly as calling out by telephone was restricted by the volume of incoming calls. Staff were mobilised from other parts of the hospital as could be spared. The unit secretary Catherine McVey came from home to organise the record keeping to identify those involved in the Ibrox incident as separate from the other casual patients and also to liase with the police. Unidentified patients were known by sequential numbering. Among those senior staff who arrived instinctively were a Consultant Anaesthetist, Dr Freda Fleming and Consultant Neurosurgeon, Mr John Turner.

The recently built Rehabilitation Unit was used as a temporary mortuary and in part as an interview facility for the police. Bed vacancies were identified and those who required in-patient treatment were dispatched to appropriate wards. Operating theatres were quickly put on stand-by. At that time there were only limited intensive care beds for surgical patients so it was fortunate that the new Institute for Neurological Sciences could accommodate appropriate patients.

As the acutely ill patients were quickly moved to their appropriate definitive care wards, the remaining injured were progressively treated in the A&E department. By 7.00pm the situation was under control and staff on duty in the hospital could return to their own units. Problems after this were of a logistical nature and concerned mainly the liaison with the police and communication staff as there were many travellers searching for friends and associates.

The event of January 1971 followed similar incidents on Stairway 13 in the 1960s since which time Bill Sillar and I had considered and planned for the response necessary to prepare for 'major incidents' as we were aware of the limitations of our existing facilities and that there was much room for improvement. Bill led the way in harnessing the drive for 'readiness' and was instrumental in setting up the first 'Action for Disaster' conference which was held in the new Walton Conference Centre at the SGH attended by disciplines involved in the subject. It created a great deal of interest since the night before it took place we were involved in the management of the 'Gower Street Rail Crash'.

Bill Sillar later went with Dr Cyril Bainbridge, Chief Medical Officer of the then Western Regional Hospital Board in Glasgow, on a tour of disaster management facilities in North America during the course of which much was learned about the different types of experiences which had been encountered there. It became clear that it was necessary to organise hospital response to a major incident so that, where it was necessary for staff to be called to an incident site, they should not be from the hospital to which the casualties would be taken but rather to a predesignated hospital alerted and prepared to receive them and supported by overflow locations should the need arise. There is no doubt that the 1971 Ibrox disaster and Glasgow's response to it was the catalyst for national heart-searching as to being prepared for the possibility of a disaster.

Matthew Reid was a 19-year-old college student whose ambition was to enter teacher training. He attended the Old Firm game with his father, also called Matt, and his friend 'Ackie' Cunningham.

On 2 January 1971 we set off to go to the game at Ibrox from our home in Caldercruix. We were all cheery and waved to my mother not knowing it would be three months later before I would return home. It would also be the last time my mother and father would see one another. For years I carried a feeling of guilt because I bought the tickets for a game of football at which my father died and my mother lost her husband. A reasonable person would say it is silly to blame yourself but I did. Lots of relatives and friends who lost someone would have had similar thoughts.

It has been said that the exit at Stairway 13 was an accident waiting to happen. This is probably correct. When fans would approach the exit from different directions and then suddenly be upon a very steep and long stairway. It would only have taken one person to fall and someone to stop and help. Any other fans following would have great difficulty stopping, as they would not know what was happening ahead. I believe that is what caused the disaster that day. The number of deaths would have been a lot less if it was not for the tall fence that ran parallel to the Stairway. If it had not been there, the fans would have been able to spill over to the side of the stairs, of this I have no doubt. A lot of people did manage to get over the fence, most of them with the help of people pulling them up from the other side and some being pushed up and over from the stairs side.

I have no recollection of any details of the game itself. I know the game ended in a draw but after the final whistle the details are very vivid. When the game finished we made our way from midway behind the goals to the back wall at the top of the terracing. We then made our way to exit 13. It was at this point that we became aware that something was wrong. My father was walking behind me with his hand on my shoulder. I knew he was concerned about my safety as I was disabled with two artificial legs. The closer we got to the Stairway the crushing became more severe and at one point we were swept off our feet and carried along and round the corner to the top of the stair next to the fence. A sudden surge took us down the stairs. I managed to get a hold of the fence. My friend Ackie, was trying to climb the fence but kept falling down. It was then something gave way; it was the handrail to my left. There was lots of screaming and a lot of people were swept away; my father was one of them. As he fell, he cried out, "Christ, my boy!" I have heard him call out many times over the years. I never saw him again. I was losing my grip of the fence and as I was going down I gave Ackie a push on his backside and he managed to get over. I went face down on the stairs; fans were walking over the top of me and no one could help this as they were being pushed from behind.

I recall one person stepping on my back and I remember thinking how heavy he was. It was at this point that I was sick. The pie and Bovril I had before the game did not taste as good the second time around. To this day, when Bovril is mentioned, it reminds me of Stairway 13. I started to pass out. I felt very peaceful and thought, 'this is it'. When I came round, I found myself on my back and facing up the stairs. Somehow I had been turned all the way around. People were lying on top of me, not moving. I was having trouble breathing. There was a small gap between the people on top of me, which was allowing air to get to me. I could hear sounds of sirens and what appeared to be oxygen being given to people. It was then I began to panic as I could hear voices saying, 'this one's dead!' I managed to squeeze my arm through the gap to try to let someone know that I was here. It was then that I began to pass out again. I realised I was cutting off my supply of air so I pulled my arm back and waited, hoping the people on top of me would not move and stop my oxygen.

When the rescuers got up as far as me, I was very relieved. Two of the people on top of me were not so fortunate. On finding me below them, a Glasgow policeman got down beside me and supported my head with his arm, then he started to cry. It was a very emotional time. I was taken to the Southern General Hospital. I lay on the trolley waiting for treatment, a few hours had passed and I was concerned as to the whereabouts of my father. Then I saw a face I knew well. It was Mr Whitefield, the doctor who had looked after me since my childhood and carried out all my operations including amputating my feet. I was taken to theatre for treatment on my right femur and then transferred to Ward 18 where I had been many times before and where I would spend the next three months.

Lying in hospital for so long gave me a lot of time to think. Not being able to go to my father's funeral was the worst day and, as I have mentioned, the self blame for buying the tickets. I still had a very difficult day to overcome. The physical scars were healing but the mental ones were just beginning. I was going home to a house that would never be the same again. I think, for the people who took part in the rescue – Willie Waddell, Jock Stein and everyone who had carried the dead to where they were lain from corner flag to goal post was something they would never get over. It was also a most harrowing thing that relatives would have to do on the evening of 2 January. They had to make their way to hospitals and mortuaries, like my two brothers Johnnie and Tommy had to do. They found out that I was in the Southern General but had difficulty tracing my father as there was no identification on him as with a lot of the victims, their clothes having been torn off due to the massive crushing which had taken place. He was finally found about 4.00am on Sunday in one of the mortuaries.

There was no such thing as counselling in those days, you just had to dust yourself down and get on with it. One of the most difficult things over the years I had trouble coping with was, if I was out somewhere, someone, usually a total stranger, would make a point of telling me that their cousin or some distant relative was 'at that game that day!' I would have loved to have been the one person to say I was not 'at that game that day!'

There were so many victims not all of them died that day. For example, the parents of the two brothers from Slamannan whose graves could be seen from their house. Sadly, both parents died within a short time of their sons. They never got over their tragic loss, just like my distraught mother. A part of all of us died that day.

It was almost 30 years later that I thought I had come to terms with things. I was on a radio programme and was shocked when one question I was asked almost floored me. The interviewer asked me what was the worst moment of all. The image which I had blanked out for all those years was when the screens were closed around my bed in the hospital the day after the game. A few minutes later they were opened and a policeman, holding his hat, was standing at my bed. Words were not necessary.

CHAPTER FIVE

AFTERMATH

By early evening, Glasgow was in a confused state of shock and numbness. Relations and friends across Scotland waited desperately for news of those they knew had attended the game at Ibrox. Agonising minutes turned to desperately long hours before hope for many became extinguished. Disbelief at the appalling loss of life on Stairway 13 would be replaced by emotions of inconsolable grief. It was beyond comprehension that many Rangers supporters had set off for Ibrox Stadium that day to support their team and yet, were never to return.

Wordsmiths began the unsavoury task of reporting loss of life and detailing those who lay injured in hospital beds. Glasgow's two daily newspapers – *The Daily Record* and *The Glasgow Herald* – together with the *Evening Times* and *Evening Citizen*, would be filled with considerable column inches about the tragedy in the days which lay ahead. Long before the advent of a slick public relations machine, it was Rangers Manager, Willie Waddell who took responsibility for the issuing of statements for consumption by a hungry media. The main question on the lips of journalists and public alike was what had caused the deaths of 66 people and left almost 150 others injured in hospital. Waddell's initial reaction was to declare that the tragedy had been caused 'by sheer public excitement due to the state of the game which was at a stage when either club could have won. This resulted in a situation which no one could have catered for.'[1]

Other theories were hastily put forward. Maureen Oswell, a resident of a fourth floor tenement flat in Cairnlea Drive, directly opposite Stairway 13, recalled that she had seen a supporter carrying another upon his shoulders before he stumbled, causing both fans to fall. A further theory, from an unknown source, was also proposed in the aftermath of the accident and then subsequently perpetuated with regular monotony into the 21st century. Suggestions were made that a number of Rangers supporters had begun to descend Stairway 13 immediately after the Celtic goal was scored. When Colin Stein equalised for Rangers close to full-time, it was proposed that those who were descending the staircase turned back up the stairs to re-enter the terraces upon hearing the Rangers fans celebratory cheering. A human collision was mooted, caused by a head-on clash of those coming down the Stairway and those climbing back up it. A later inquiry would reject such a proposal although the tired myth would continue to be perpetuated in the years to come and indeed, it continues to surface to the present day.

Meanwhile, telephone enquiries were received at the Central Police office in Glasgow from friends and relations desperate for news about those who attended the Rangers – Celtic match. Calls came not only from Scotland but also from other parts of Britain, Australia, Canada and America. Police staff worked well beyond their shift time to deal with the influx of calls, which had topped the thousand mark by noon the next day. A senior police officer announced, 'We have had a great number of calls from England and from abroad asking if persons who usually or sometimes go to the Old Firm games were among the dead or injured. This increases the work we have to do.'[2]

Many relatives called at the police station in person and were invited to wait in the Central Police Court because of the freezing Glasgow weather. Chillingly, at intervals, a list of the bodies which had been identified, was read out to those who had gathered. Other relatives of the dead and those who had failed to come home visited the city mortuary in the wake of the tragedy. Some who had travelled from further afield to identify bodies were accommodated and comforted at a Salvation Army hostel in the city. Reaction, inevitably, was one of numbness and tears.

News of the Ibrox Disaster spread across the world and messages of sympathy were hastily issued. In Rome, Pope Paul declared, 'We have present in our hearts the dead and injured in the terrible disaster in Glasgow.'[3] The New Zealand Prime Minister, Sir Keith Holyoaks, also expressed his sorrow and forwarded a message stating that all New Zealanders were deeply distressed by the tragedy. Further messages of condolence were sent by President Nixon of America and German Chancellor, Willy Brandt. Sympathy and comment in Glasgow was also quickly forthcoming. A spokesman for the Sikh community announced that prayers had been said for the souls of the Ibrox victims at their temple in Nithsdale Road in neighbouring Pollockshields. Celtic manager, Jock Stein solemnly announced, 'Words cannot express feelings at a time like this. No one is feeling like football at the moment.'[4] James White, MP for Pollock, said, 'I have been at games before with my young son and we have been carried by the crowd down these same steps. It is only by the grace of God it has not happened before this.'[5] Sir Donald Liddle, Lord Provost of

Glasgow, who had watched the game from the Directors' box pronounced, 'It is extremely difficult even yet to realise the enormity of the disaster which has hit Glasgow.'[6] Sir Donald himself had tried to comfort the injured. He had experienced at first hand the magnitude of the disaster; the dozens of shoes which had been torn off, the moaning people scattered on and around the Stairway and, most tragically of all, the bodies covered with jackets and coats. As the dead had been lifted away, coins were heard falling from the pockets of those who had perished. Lord Provost James McKay of Edinburgh, sent a telegram to his Glasgow counterpart stating he was 'Deeply shocked to learn of the tragedy at Ibrox,'[7] and 'At this stage, all assistance which our city can give, is freely offered. Please convey to relatives of those killed and injured our deepest sympathy.'[8]

Before Sir Donald left the eerie stadium on that bitterly cold Saturday night, he launched the Ibrox Disaster fund to help the dependant relatives of the deceased and those who would suffer financial hardship due to injuries, which they had sustained in the accident. Rangers immediately contributed £50,000, Celtic £10,000 and other clubs and organisations generously followed. £1000 was given by Manchester United, £2000 was gifted by the Scottish Co-operative Wholesale Society Ltd., £5000 from Mecca Ltd, and £500 from the British Olivetti Company. Former Rangers idol, the late Jim Baxter, arranged a collection at his public house at Paisley Road Toll and quickly raised more than £500 with the first donation of £10 coming from a Celtic supporter. Rangers and Celtic supporters associations later issued a joint statement asking their respective members to contribute to the disaster fund. Collection boxes were later placed in supporters social clubs and public houses. Hibernian Supporters Association donated £100 to the fund and Shotts Bon Accord Football and Social Club raised a further £50. Further afield, in Uries, Holland, a fund raising campaign was launched to help relatives of those who had died at Ibrox. The initiative was taken by the Dutch who recalled the fine hospitality many of their countrymen had enjoyed in Glasgow during the Second World War. The Mayor of Belfast, Alderman JS Cairns, also announced he was launching a disaster fund with a personal donation of £100. Willie Waddell, in a prepared statement, later declared,' At their meeting today the Directors of Rangers Football Club expressed their deep sorrow and heartfelt sympathy for the bereaved relatives of those who lost their lives and for those who were injured at Ibrox Stadium on Saturday.'[9] He added, 'They have decided to donate the sum of £50,000 to the Lord Provost's appeal fund. The Directors also expressed their grateful thanks and admiration for the heroic efforts of the police, ambulance personnel, doctors, nurses and hospital staffs, fire brigade, personnel of both Celtic and Rangers Football Clubs and members of the public who came to the assistance of the victims of this terrible disaster.'[10]

Sympathy, support and assistance were soon received from the wider football community. Sir Stanley Rous, President of FIFA, commented, 'On behalf of world football, I send my deepest sympathy. It is terrible that this has happened at Ibrox, a good ground.'[11] Dr Helmut Kaiser, secretary of FIFA, was shocked at news of the accident and declared, 'What a tragedy that such a disaster should hit football.'[12]

Chairman of the English FA, Dr Andrew Stephen, announced, 'It is dreadful. A terrible moment in football.'[13] Practical assistance was forthcoming from Europe and beyond. Valencia manager and former Real Madrid legend, Alfredo Di Stefano, spoke emotionally and declared, 'We sympathise with Rangers in this awful tragedy and would like to help the relatives of the victims.'[14] His Spanish Club offered to play the Glasgow team anywhere, at any time and without cost. An official of Portuguese giants Benfica stated, 'We have had players from Rangers and Celtic here to play in a benefit for one of our players just a few weeks ago. If we are asked, then you can take it as 99 per cent that Eusebio or any other of our players would be privileged to take part in a match in aid of the disaster.'[15] A West German FA spokesman declared, 'We have a good relationship with Scottish football and, in particular, with Rangers who have played here so often. If we are asked to help we will try to do so. I do not wish to make hollow promises ... but can assure you, if a suitable date is arranged which would allow German stars to take part in any such match, then we would do everything we could to help. We have been stunned by this tragedy.'[16] Further comment was forthcoming from a representative of the Italian FA who stated, 'It is for everyone to co-operate in such tragic circumstances.'[17] Manchester rivals, United and City, made offers to stage a fund-raising game, while in South America, a representative of the Brazilian FA declared, 'I have already sent a letter of sympathy to the Scottish Football Association. My Association in Brazil is deeply upset about this disaster and I am certain that any request for our players would be met sympathetically. Naturally the clubs would have the main say about the release of players but the Association would do as much as possible to assist. To aid a cause like this is an honour in itself.'[18] Offers of support and help were both well meaning and considerable but attention for many, remained focused on what had caused the death and injury of more than 200 people on the steps of Stairway 13 at Ibrox Stadium.

The day after the accident, Gordon Campbell, Secretary of State for

Scotland, visited the Rangers ground. At a Press Conference, he commented 'Appalling as this disaster was it could have been considerably worse if pressure on those who did not know what was happening had not been held and siphoned off elsewhere.'[19] He added,' I hope to announce within a few days what type of inquiry will be held. There is more than one form of inquiry and there could be more than one in this case. I shall get a full report tomorrow on what courses are open to me.'[20] The following day, Mr Campbell flew to London to present a personal report of the disaster to Mr Edward Heath, the Prime Minister. The response of the Government was to announce the setting up of two inquiries, the first being a fatal accident inquiry, followed by an inquiry into safety at all sports fixtures across Britain. The inquiries would take place in the future – Glasgow for now though, was more concerned with the present. It proved to be encouraging news that 130 supporters of the 145 who had been injured at Ibrox had been allowed to leave hospital the day following the disaster.

CHAPTER SIX

TORNADO OF GRIEF

The flags, which flew at half-mast in Glasgow in the wake of the Ibrox disaster, made for a sorrowful sight. The city meanwhile attempted to come to terms with the deaths of 66 people and the others that lay injured in hospital beds. Football became insignificant as the dreadful loss of life became ever more sharply focused. Rangers cancelled a mid-week trip to Spain where they had been due to play Valencia in a friendly. After consultation with the Scottish League, the Ibrox club also postponed both first team and reserve fixtures against Cowdenbeath the following Saturday. Rangers manager, Willie Waddell, declared that his players were 'visibly shaken'[1] by the events of 2 January and said that each had been given a list of relatives of the dead, located in their respective areas. It was the club's intention to be represented at every funeral. The Lord Provost of Glasgow, Sir Donald Liddle, stated 'every relative of victims will be visited by social workers within the coming week.'[2] As a further mark of respect, Glasgow adversaries Celtic and Clyde called off their re-arranged New Year's Day fixture which had been due to be played at Parkhead two days after the Old Firm clash.

The first Monday of January 1971 marked the start of a traumatic and intense period for the players and officials of Rangers Football Club. Alfie Conn, John Greig, Willie Henderson, Colin Jackson, Sandy Jardine, Willie Johnston, Derek Johnstone, Willie Mathieson, Ronnie McKinnon, Gerry Neef, Andy Penman, Dave Smith, Colin Stein and Robert Watson together with the coach, Jock Wallace, physiotherapist, Tommy Craig and club doctor Dr Donald Cruikshank were a sizeable party which visited the injured at two Glasgow hospitals. The Ibrox contingent first visited the Victoria Infirmary and talked to six survivors of the disaster. They heard anecdotes of miraculous escapes and chilling eyewitness accounts. Cigarettes, fruit and sweets were distributed; probably little more than a distraction but undoubtedly well meaning under the circumstances. The party later visited nine injured supporters at the Southern General Hospital where the same sympathetic procedure was repeated.

It was solemn mourners and not gleeful supporters who lined the aisles four deep, five days into January of 1971. St Andrews Roman Catholic Cathedral in Glasgow was shrouded in sadness as Mass was offered by Archbishop James Donald Scanlon for those who lost their lives at Ibrox Stadium. Directors, officials, players and managers of Rangers and Celtic football clubs were interwoven in a congregation of some 1200 people who had gathered to pay their respects to the victims of Stairway 13. Chief Constable Sir James Robertson, magistrates, councillors, MPs and members of the ambulance, police and hospital services, who had been involved in rescue work three days earlier, were all present. In addressing the assembled congregation, Archbishop Scanlon said in his sermon: 'In offering this Mass today, we of the Catholic community are paying the highest tribute in our power to the victims of Saturday's appalling disaster. Glasgow, as the Pope has stated, has been plunged into mourning at a time when happiness and rejoicing were expected. The deaths of so many in the flower of youth would have tragic repercussions, which would be a lifetime's memory. For us who can scarcely feel the full impact of this tornado of grief, there is surely a lesson. Always it is the things which affect us outwardly and impress themselves on our senses that are the shams, the imaginaries; reality belongs to the things of the spirit.' He added, 'A disaster of Saturday's magnitude and immediacy strips us of the illusion that the world is permanent.'[3] Journalist and television commentator, Bob Crampsey, read the first lesson from the Old Testament while Celtic footballer, Jim Craig, read a further one from the New Testament. William Dunn, Chairman of Clyde Football Club, David McParland and Sean Fallon, Manager and Assistant Manager of Partick Thistle Football Club took part in the offertory procession. The service was moving although the atmosphere was sombre.

Scenes of melancholy were to be repeated on 9 January when civic dignitaries, players and officials of Rangers and Celtic were amongst a congregation of some 3,000 mourners who gathered at Glasgow Cathedral to hear a service conducted by Reverend Dr William Morris. It was Ibrox Parish Minister, Robert Bone, though who paid a deserving tribute to the players of Rangers and Celtic by declaring,' We remember with pride these young men who share in the grief of all the bereaved. They have seen in a week as much sorrow as many do in a lifetime.'[4] Flags on government buildings in Scotland flew at half-mast on that sombre Saturday as the nation mourned its dead.

The four successive days from Wednesday 6 until Saturday 9 January proved to be among the darkest days in the history of Rangers Football Club. True to the club's word though, they were represented at each of the funerals, which took place not only in Glasgow but also in Edinburgh, Lanarkshire, Argyll, Fife, Renfrewshire, Stirlingshire, Dunbartonshire and East Lothian. Players and club officials made a succession of appearances as shuttle services were provided to ferry those with a Rangers connection to the funerals. The service for David McGhee, however, was private and Rangers made their representation by sending a lone wreath. Six funerals took place on the Wednesday, 40 on the Thursday, 18 on the Friday and two on the Saturday; one of which was for the youngest victim, nine-year-old Nigel Pickup whose funeral was held in Huyton, Liverpool. Fate dealt a cruel blow to the youngster as he had attended the Rangers-Celtic game with his step-father, David McPherson. They had flown in specially from Edmonton, Canada to see the game. Sadly, both were to lose their lives. The oldest victim was Matthew Reid from Caldercruix who was 49 when he perished.

The endless funerals brought home the numbing reality of the tragedy, which had occurred, on the steps of Stairway 13. Margaret Ferguson, from Maddiston, Falkirk was just 18 and the only female to lose her life in the disaster. Almost half of the 66 fans who died were in their teenage years. Amongst them were five boys from the small village of Markinch in Fife. Peter Easton (13), Martin Paton (14), Mason Phillips (14), Brian Todd (14) and Douglas Morrison (15). The friends, who were regular attendees at Rangers games, all came from the same street; Park View and its continuation, George Street. The youngsters had all been members of the Glenrothes Rangers Supporters Club and had played for the same local football team. Tragically, the five boys were the only passengers who had failed to return to their supporters' bus after the game. Rangers sent the same six-man delegation – Chairman John Lawrence and players Alfie Conn, Willie Johnston, Derek Johnstone, Billy Mathieson and Andy Penman to the boy's funerals in Markinch and Kirkcaldy, which took place on the afternoon of Thursday 7 January. The harrowing spectacle was to be repeated across the country. Brothers Richard and John McLeay (28 years and 32 years old respectively) were part of a joint funeral service held in their hometown of Slammanan, Stirlingshire on the morning of that bleak Thursday. The next day, Royal Engineer James McGovern (24), from Tranent was buried with full military honours. He was not alone in leaving behind a young family who had to try to understand and come to terms with terrible loss. Everyone associated with Rangers Football Club had been subjected to the severest of emotional batterings during the early days of 1971 and yet, somehow, the Glasgow club had to pull itself up by its frayed bootlaces and attempt to return to some semblance of normality. Two weeks after the Old Firm game, Ibrox Stadium, with some reluctance, opened its turnstiles for business.

On Saturday 16 January, Willie Johnston replaced Derek Johnstone in an otherwise un-changed Rangers team to face Dundee United in a league fixture. A metaphorical black cloud descended on Ibrox that afternoon as a tangible sadness enveloped the vast stadium. Players surrounded the centre circle with heads bowed and joined the 27,776 spectators in observing a two minute silence for those who had been victims of the Ibrox disaster. The passionless game on the park came a poor second to the doleful emotions off it. The match finished in a 1-1 draw but it was the occasion and not the result, which mattered that day. Stairway 13 remained closed and silent. Flowers and wreaths lay at the bottom of the vast expanse of concrete steps; they made for a sorrowful sight.

CHAPTER SEVEN

OLD FIRM UNITED

Three and a half weeks after Rangers and Celtic had met in their epoch making encounter, Glasgow geared up for another heavyweight fixture. The old rivals though, were not to face each other but were to combine in a resolute unit. On the evening of 27 January, a Rangers-Celtic Select team came face to face with a Scotland X1 at Hampden Park. An abundance of British talent was on show although the ultimate winner would be the Ibrox Disaster Fund, which would reap the proceeds from the takings at the gate. The occasion was to appeal greatly to the city's football supporters as 81,405 spectators filed through the turnstiles to see a collection of Scots, two Englishmen and an Irishman ply their trade. The prospect was mouth watering and the match itself did not disappoint.

Eight Rangers and Celtic players who had appeared in the New Year Ibrox fixture were in the starting line-ups at Hampden and this number would have been further swelled but for the withdrawal of Celtic's Jimmy Johnstone. The Parkhead winger had injured himself two days prior to the game after gashing his foot on broken glass. His replacement was clubmate John Hughes, known affectionately to the Celtic faithful as 'Big Yogi'. It made for an interesting though unusual sight to see Chelsea's Peter Bonetti behind a strong Rangers-Celtic backline. The English contingent was further strengthened by the addition of the majestic Bobby Charlton. The long serving Manchester United star had commented prior to his appearance at Hampden Park: 'I am thrilled to be asked. Just tell me when you want me and where.'[1] Charlton's team-mate, George Best was also delighted to be involved. Though having recently made one of his infamous disappearing acts and being subsequently suspended by his club, Best had declared, 'It was great to be invited to take part in this game. I am certainly going out at Hampden to enjoy myself.'[2] Manager for the evening, Willie Waddell, would surely have loved to have had the two Old Trafford stalwarts on the Rangers payroll. He declared, 'The show of goodwill has broken all barriers of nationality and creeds.'[3]

Scotland manager, Bobby Brown, was also able to field a powerful line-up.

The national side was faced with an important European Nations Cup game against Belgium in Liege the following Wednesday but the unexpected Hampden fixture gave Brown the opportunity to fine tune team tactics against strong domestic opposition. Nine of his Scotland team were full internationals and while Archie Gemmill and Peter Lorimer were still awaiting their senior debuts, both had been capped at under 23 level. All 11 players in the Rangers-Celtic Select side were full internationals and although it was a scratch side, it was one which commanded the respect of the opposition.

The game started brightly as the four pronged Rangers-Celtic Select forward line of Best, Henderson, Hughes and Johnston went on the offensive against a Scottish defensive line of Hay, McKinnon, Moncur and Gemmell. Driven forward by the midfield guile of Charlton and Murdoch, Hughes' attempted pass to Johnston was almost swept into his own goal by the covering Bobby Moncur in the opening minute. The frantic rearguard action continued when the lively Henderson had a powerful shot well saved by Jim Cruikshank in the Scotland goal. The national side weathered the initial ten minute storm when, against the run of play, the Scotland XI broke away for Colin Stein to square the ball to Archie Gemmill, who fired home from the edge of the penalty area. Bobby Charlton continued to prompt from midfield and sprayed passes across the Hampden surface in sublime fashion. A century of England caps to his name, Charlton's long passing was truly awesome. Willie Henderson weaved his magic and was determined not to be outshone by the impish Best on the opposite flank. Colin Stein continually backtracked the Irish wing wizard although neither he nor any of his Scottish team-mates could prevent Best from firing home a blistering equaliser from Henderson's free-kick after 29 minutes. The long-haired Irishman further demonstrated his abundant skill by beating four defenders during a breathtaking run, only to shoot narrowly wide of goal.

Seventy minutes into the game, Charlie Cooke crossed, only for Peter Lorimer to head wide of the goal from five yards out. Ten minutes later, the Rangers-Celtic Select had a goal disallowed after Hughes and Charlton had linked up only to see the Englishman's effort ruled out because of an infringement. Scotland XI responded in the 84th minute when John O'Hare laid the ball to Peter Lorimer whose low shot beat Peter Bonetti. Lorimer's goal proved to be the match winner although the true victor was the Ibrox Disaster Fund, which was swelled by £40,000 thanks to the generosity of Glasgow's match-going public. Fittingly, both the Rangers and Celtic supporters, at their respective ends of the ground, gave both teams a justified standing ovation as they left the Hampden pitch.

THE TEAMS

Rangers-Celtic Select		Scotland XI
Peter Bonetti (Chelsea)	1.	Jim Cruickshank (Hearts)
Sandy Jardine (Rangers)	2.	David Hay (Celtic)
John Greig (Rangers) Capt.	3.	Tommy Gemmell (Celtic)
Bobby Murdoch (Celtic)	4.	Pat Stanton (Hibernian)
Billy McNeill (Celtic)	5.	Ron McKinnon (Rangers)
Dave Smith (Rangers)	6.	Bobby Moncur (Newcastle Utd) Capt.
Willie Henderson (Rangers)	7.	Peter Lorimer (Leeds Utd)
John Hughes (Celtic)	8.	Archie Gemmill (Derby County)
Bobby Charlton (Manchester Utd)	9.	Colin Stein (Rangers)
Willie Johnston (Rangers)	10.	John O'Hare (Derby County)
George Best (Manchester Utd)	11.	Charlie Cooke (Chelsea)
		Subs
		Jim Craig (Celtic)
		for McKinnon
		Tommy McLean (Rangers)
		for Lorimer

Referee
W Anderson (East Kilbride)

Linesmen
W McFarlane (Bonnybridge)
WH Quinn (Stewarton)

CHAPTER EIGHT

THE INQUIRY

The fatal accident inquiry into the Ibrox disaster opened at Pollockshaws Burgh Hall, three miles south of Glasgow City centre on Monday, 15 February 1971. The tragic event at Ibrox Stadium would be examined in meticulous detail and yet this would inevitably bring forth the painful re-opening of the wounds that had scarcely had time to heal. Pollockshaws became the focus of considerable attention as the inquiry would last seven days. In excess of 100 witnesses were cited and more than 1000 statements which had been taken by the police were available during the course of the hearing held before Sir Allan Walker, QC, Sheriff of Lanarkshire.

Mr David Brand QC, and Solicitor General with Mr Harry Herron, procurator fiscal, led the evidence for the Crown. The insurers of Ibrox Stadium were represented by Mr Robert Johnston QC, Dean of Faculty of Advocates and Rangers Football Club were represented by Mr WR Grieve QC. The relatives of those who were killed in the disaster were represented by more than 20 solicitors plus six senior and junior counsel. The Law Society of Scotland had been instructed to offer free legal advice to relatives who had not employed their own solicitors. Members of the emergency services, hospital authorities and Glasgow Corporation were also present.

On the first day of the inquiry, eyewitness Robert Duncan, whose tenement flat overlooked Stairway 13, declared that he regularly watched crowds leaving by this exit after big matches. He felt that if it had not been for the actions of the police in sealing off the top part of the Stairway, then the number of deaths would have been much higher. He added that it was not unusual for people to leave the stadium without touching a step due to the pressure of the crowd and steepness of the stairs. Mr Duncan went on to say that he had seen a young man carrying a jacket who went down and that people were then falling over each other. There was a pile of bodies which was three or four feet deep, which was bursting the side of the railings. He continued to describe the graphic and frantic rescue scene and the speed in which the police had acted. Somewhat controversially, Mr Duncan made the point that he considered there would have been no disaster had it not been for Rangers late equalising goal.

On that first day of evidence, a fellow resident of Cairnlea Drive, Mrs Maureen Oswell, stated that she often watched supporters leaving the east terracing via the Stairway 13 route and had witnessed two previous incidents on the stair in 1961 and 1969. She mentioned that at the end of the 2 January 1971 game, some supporters had begun to leave the stadium after Celtic had scored. When Rangers equalised, Mrs Oswell stated that supporters stopped on the Stairway upon hearing the celebratory roar and joined in the celebrations – cheering and waving their arms in the air and then continuing their descent. They made no attempt to climb back up. She also stated that she had seen a youth sitting on a man's shoulders and she had remarked to her husband that she felt it was a stupid thing to do. Mrs Oswell continued that the two had disappeared from her view and that everyone was moving forward and starting to fall. She felt that it was as if a hole had appeared in the ground and that people were falling into it. Mrs Oswell commented that people tried to tear down the wooden fencing at the side of the Stairway but could not move it as it was too strong. In her opinion, the incident had been caused by the youth sitting on the man's shoulders, although she stressed she had not seen anyone actually stumble.

Professor Giles Forbes, of the chair of forensic medicine at Glasgow University had earlier stated that both he and Dr William McClay, the Glasgow police medical officer, had examined all of the 66 bodies from the disaster and that 60 had died of asphyxiation caused by outside pressure and six had died from suffocation which had been due to their air passages being blocked.

Mr Thomas Tinto, co-ordinator of the Ibrox disaster fund, stated that 21 payments amounting to more than £2,000 had been made to relatives of some of the deceased. Some relatives had received a grant of £100 whilst other relatives had funeral accounts reimbursed from the fund.

Day two of the inquiry consisted of eyewitness accounts from spectators who had been caught up in the disaster. Mr James Brown, for example, spoke of the intense pressure of the crowd and described it as 'the worst I had known in my experience of frequently attending these matches.'[1] He continued, 'The press of the crowd above was so great that I couldn't get my arms free to assist a man who was jammed against the metal fence down the Stairway.'[2] Fellow spectator, John Williamson declared, 'When I was leaving the stadium on 2 January, I heard shouting and swearing from behind. When I looked, I saw heaps of people; a mass of bodies everywhere. It started on the landing and spread.'[3] Disturbingly, the majority of those who died on the Stairway had been found without shoes, suggesting that the pressure of the crowd had been intense.

Day three of the inquiry included further descriptive evidence from supporters and accounts from police officers that had been present at the game. Sergeant Donald Bottom, who on the day of the game had been a constable, described the dreadful scene of the bodies; 'They appeared to be leaning forward. Their arms were trapped by their sides and their heads were either facing the bottom of the Stairway or resting on the shoulders and backs of those in front.'[4]

Chief Superintendent Purdon who had supervised the duties of fellow officers on the day of the game, mentioned that the stewarding had been the sole responsibility of Rangers Football Club but under his control on that day he had 330 constables and officers as well as 33 special policemen and 48 traffic wardens which was in excess of the ratio stipulated by the Lang committee on ground safety requirements. The chief superintendent had supervised the removal of the casualties from the Stairway, which had taken half an hour. The day after the Old Firm game he had examined the scene and the terraces and observed the large number of beer cans and wine bottles, although he did not think that there had been any more drinking than was normal for the New Year derby.

On day four, Mr J. Scotland Symon, then General Manager of Partick Thistle and previously manager of Rangers between 1954 and 1967, stated that Stairway 13 had been altered and improved after the accident in 1961 in which two spectators had lost their lives and described Ibrox Stadium as 'one of the best club football grounds in Europe.'[5] Rangers had six handrails installed on the Stairway which thus divided it into seven separate lanes and also had the stairs concreted. Mr Symon commented, 'It was felt that the erection of the handrails would reduce crowd pressure in each lane.'[6] He was also in agreement with Mr WR Grieve, for Rangers Football Club, that two court actions had been brought by relatives of the two supporters who had perished in 1961 but neither case had been successful as no fault could be apportioned to the Ibrox club. The depute master of works and city engineer of Glasgow Corporation, William Greer, also giving evidence that day, said that he had examined Stairway 13 and observed that two sections of a metal banister had been broken and two more sections had been bent. He declared, 'This was a substantial railing. It was a good staircase.'[7]

On day five, David Hope, then a director of Rangers Football Club stated that the Ibrox board of directors had considered the safety of Stairway 13 after a previous incident in 1969 which had resulted in the injury to 30 spectators that afternoon. After due consideration though, the Rangers board felt that they were satisfied with the existing arrangements for the

Stairway. Mr Hope further added that he had no recollection of a meeting after the incident in 1969 at which officials of Rangers Football Club, who were accompanied by inspectors from the Master of Works department of Glasgow Corporation, had made recommendations that there should be an alteration of the stairway handrails so as to allow the flow of the supporters to 'fan out' as they made their way out of the ground. Whilst Mr Hope stated he had no recollection of the meeting, he did acknowledge that it could have taken place and that, indeed, he could have been present.

The sixth day of evidence was given on 22 February 1971. On that Monday, Mr John Lawrence, chairman of Rangers Football Club spoke, declaring that he and his fellow directors were 'tremendously concerned'[8] that the accident on 2 January 1971 had been the fourth to occur in less than ten years on Stairway 13 and yet, since the first accident in 1961, £150,000 had been spent on improvements to the stadium.

Mr Lawrence further added that after the first accident on 16 September 1961, the Scottish Football Association had made general recommendations to clubs that each should endeavour to improve ground safety. He said Rangers had consulted a firm of civil engineers and that alterations and repairs had been carried out.

Mr Andrew Sproull, a consulting civil engineer, was also called to give evidence and he stated that his firm had carried out work on Stairway 13 in 1962. This had consisted of cementing over earth and sleeper steps as well as erecting six sets of tubular metal handrails which formed seven, six feet wide passageways.

Fifty-two days after the Old Firm derby which had claimed the lives of 66 football supporters, the verdict at the fatal accident inquiry was given. After two and a half hours of deliberations, the jury of four men and three women found that those who had died in the wake of the 2 January game, had done so as a consequence of being crushed or covered by the bodies of other persons. The evidence suggested that the accident had been caused because one or more persons had fallen or collapsed on the Stairway. Those who had been moving down the Stairway were solidly packed together and were being forced downwards by the pressure of others behind them.

The statement which was read by the foreman of the jury stated, 'The downward pressure of the crowd above, forced other persons to fall or collapse on those who had fallen first and as the downward pressure continued, more and more persons were heaped upon those who had fallen or were pressed hard against them.'[9] Such a rational conclusion put to bed the fallacy about the human collision supposedly caused by supporters climbing back up the Stairway and colliding with others coming down.

Furthermore, the jury of seven stated that deaths were always likely to happen on Stairway 13 in its present condition if a densely packed mass of people continued to descend the staircase and recommended that expert advice should be taken by Rangers Football Club about reducing the number of people using Stairway 13 in the future. Decisively, the Ibrox club was exonerated of blame for the disaster itself.

The original Ibrox Disaster fund, set up by the then Lord Provost of Glasgow, Sir Donald Liddle, to which Rangers had contributed £50,000, was wound up in October 1971 with 23 widows sharing £137,000, 46 children sharing £118,000 and dependant parents sharing £58,000. In the wake of the fatal accident inquiry, Margaret Dougan, who had been widowed after her husband Charles died in the disaster, proceeded with a civil suit against Rangers. The action by the Clydebank widow was to culminate in her being awarded damages of £26,621 on 23 October 1974. The sum, £19,621 for Mrs Dougan and £3,500 for each of her two sons, Charles, then aged 12 and James, then aged ten was awarded by Sheriff J. Irvine Smith who, regrettably for Rangers, was scathing about the club at considerable length in a 27 page note relating to his judgement.

Sheriff Smith criticised the Ibrox Club for failing to take adequate measures to improve the exit arrangements at Stairway 13 despite three previous incidents prior to the 1971 disaster. He declared that the only conclusion which could be reached via extracts of minutes which were produced in court was 'the defenders never once in formal meeting applied their minds to the question of the causes of these accidents, never once considered that it might be desirable to take professional advice on the potential dangers of the Cairnlea Drive Stairway and would appear, I put it no higher, to have proceeded on the view that if the problem was ignored long enough, it would eventually disappear.'[10]

Sheriff Smith additionally criticised the inadequacy of the written records of the Rangers board relating to the action which could be taken over the period the accidents had happened. He declared, 'Rarely can an organisation of the size and significance of Rangers Football Club have succeeded in conducting their business with records so sparse, so carelessly kept, so inaccurately written up and so indifferently stored.'[11]

The Sheriff's award and accompanying words hit Rangers insurer, Norwich Union, financially but his sharp rebuke would probably have stung the Football Club a whole lot harder.

Stairway 13 had claimed the lives of 66 supporters in dreadful circumstances. Rangers, football and sport in general though, had learned a major lesson albeit in a most emotionally painful manner. Scottish judge,

Lord Wheatley, later headed a further inquiry into spectator safety at sports grounds which would eventually lead to the 1975 Safety of Sports Grounds Act, which stipulated that local authorities were required to issue safety certificates for any sporting arena which accommodated in excess of 10,000 spectators. Rangers meanwhile, dismantled their ground piece by piece and replaced it with a magnificent new stadium.

Disturbingly, in January 2002 documents were released by the National Archives of Scotland revealing that local councils had been refused the powers to improve safety at football grounds only six months prior to the Ibrox Disaster. The official records revealed that in July 1970, Scottish councils were informed by the Government that ground improvements which were sought only offered 'marginal benefits' and that the time was not yet right for legislation. The request for improvements had been led by council chiefs in Glasgow who, at that time had been concerned about crowd safety at Hampden Park, Parkhead and, ironically, Ibrox. Such news 31 years on caused shock and considerable upset for relatives of those who had died on Stairway 13.

CHAPTER NINE

'DEEDLE'

The thoughts of the Rangers officials remained not only with the relatives and friends of those who had perished on the steps of Stairway 13 but attention also began to turn towards crowd safety at Ibrox. The day after the disaster, Manager Willie Waddell had commented, 'The Club contends that it has one of the best maintained stadiums in Britain. Rangers have always been conscious of the high safety standards that are required.'[1] Yet it may have been such a comment which triggered Waddell's dream of a new Ibrox Stadium.

Rangers decided to act. The Club recruited a company of consulting engineers – WA Fairhurst and Partners – to observe and record minute by minute crowd movements at Ibrox, supported by aerial photographs taken by a circling aircraft during Rangers 1-0 victory against Aberdeen in the Scottish Cup 5th Round tie on 6 March 1971. Close attention, inevitably, was paid to supporters leaving the stadium on the re-opened Stairway 13. Following the observation and considerable discussion, Rangers submitted plans for alterations to Ibrox Stadium, which were approved by Glasgow Dean of Guild Court on 9 July 1971. Precise details were not disclosed at the time but it was understood that the plans covered remedial work on Stairways 1, 13 and 19. Such plans later came to fruition as large concrete walls were erected at the top of the terracing to slow down and filter supporters into a passageway leading to the stairways. Decisively, the high wooden side fencing which had restricted escape from Stairway 13 on 2 January was removed and replaced with handrails. The cost of the alterations was reported to be £12,000. A stark reminder of the lurking danger however, was a sign displayed above Stairway 13. It read simply, 'Caution. First step down.'

It was Willie Waddell though, more than anyone else at Rangers Football Club, who realised that in the longer term it was major surgery and not minor cosmetics, which was required to transform the face of Ibrox Stadium. Waddell had always had a strong influence on proceedings at Rangers although his abrasive manner was not universally welcomed.

There would be few in number, however, who would question Waddell's contribution to the Rangers cause after he signed as a professional in May 1938. As a player he proved to be highly effective and successful as a winger, bagging four league championship medals and two Scottish Cup winners medals with Rangers. Affectionately known as 'Deedle', he was also capped 17 times for Scotland. He retired at the age of 35 having played in 299 Scottish league, Scottish Cup and League Cup games for the club scoring 58 goals in the process.

Waddell moved into journalism after leaving Rangers, working first for the *Scottish Daily Mail* and later the Glasgow *Evening Citizen*. In 1957 though, he was lured back into football by minnows Kilmarnock, whose football fortunes he transformed in an eight year stay at the Ayrshire Club. The highlight of his time at Rugby Park was securing the Scottish League Championship in 1964/5 – a monumental achievement for such a small side. Dramatically, following his heroics at Kilmarnock, he quit the club and returned to journalism whereupon he joined the *Scottish Daily Express*. However, the lure of Rangers proved to be too great and he returned to the club which was closest to his heart, as manager on 3 December 1969. Under Waddell's leadership, Rangers secured the League Cup in 1970. It was the events of the evening of 24 May 1972, however, which proved to be the highlight of Deedle's managerial reign as Rangers secured the European Cup Winners Cup by beating Moscow Dynamo 3-2 in Barcelona. There remained however, one last stunning announcement from Willie Waddell. In the wake of the European success he announced on the 7 June 1972, that he planned to step down as manager of the Club to be succeeded by his assistant, Jock Wallace. Waddell, meanwhile, assumed the title of General Manager.

This new job proved to be every bit as challenging as his previous roles as a player, journalist and team manager as his thoughts turned to the transformation of Ibrox Stadium.

The man from Forth in Lanarkshire travelled widely across Europe, studying modern football stadia. He was particularly impressed with Borussia Dortmund's Westfalen Stadium, which would be used for the 1974 World Cup Finals in West Germany. It was deemed modern and above all, safe and was used as the blueprint for a modern Ibrox Stadium. In late 1977, radical plans were announced for the new Ibrox which would leave only the original main grandstand remaining. An architectural gem, the stand was designed by the eminent Glasgow-born engineer and factory architect Archibald Leitch in 1928 and was listed as Category B (the equivalent of Grade 2) in 1987.

Leitch, originally described as a Consulting Engineer and Factory Architect despite holding a mechanical engineering qualification, had also been responsible for the design of Manchester United's Old Trafford ground in 1908. He also had input into Celtic Park, Hampden Park, Highbury (Arsenal), Fratton Park (Portsmouth), Goodison Park (Everton), Anfield (Liverpool), White Hart Lane (Tottenham Hotspur), Stamford Bridge (Chelsea), Villa Park (Aston Villa), Molineux (Wolverhampton Wanderers) and Craven Cottage (Fulham) with his many designs. In August 1978, the haunting presence of Stairway 13 was finally exorcised when a bulldozer moved in to reduce the vast expanse of steps and terracing to rubble.

The transformation was dramatic. The following year, honorary director and former player, George Brown, opened the Copland Road Stand on 18 August 1979, before a 2-2 Premier League draw against Celtic. Work continued at the west end of the ground and the Copland's mirror image – the Broomloan Road Stand, opened on 4 August 1980 as Rangers defeated Tottenham Hotspur 2-1 in a challenge match. The initial rebuilding programme was completed at a cost of £10m with the opening of the Govan Stand on the north side of the ground. Willie Waddell, appropriately, officiated on 22 December 1981, before a friendly match against Liverpool – a game that resulted in a 2-0 victory for the visitors.

With further improvements and additions to the ground such as the completion of the Club Deck above the main stand in 1991 and the seating of the corner areas at the Govan Stand, Greater Ibrox stands as a fitting testament to the foresight of Willie Waddell and a memorial to those who died in the Ibrox disaster. The stadium, which now holds a capacity 50,500 spectators has been awarded UEFA five-star status.

Speaking after Willie Waddell's death on 14 October 1992, Chairman David Murray commented, 'The Club owes Willie Waddell a tremendous debt. He will be remembered not only for his playing career but also for laying the foundations of the new stadium.'[2]

CHAPTER TEN

IN MEMORIAM

One year and a day after the Ibrox Disaster, wreaths of remembrance were laid in Edinburgh and Markinch in memory of those who had died 12 months earlier.

At Ibrox, a lone wreath was laid on the terracing while across the city, Rangers prepared to take on their old rivals at Parkhead in the traditional New Year encounter.

The first anniversary inevitably, rekindled unhappy memories. The 2 January 1971 would be a date that Glasgow was destined never to forget although 20 years would pass before Rangers would unveil a commemorative plaque.

On 2 January 1991, Rangers Chairman, David Murray unveiled what many regarded as an inadequate recognition of the occasion. Sadly, there were jeers and catcalls – widely reported in the Press – by Celtic fans and a minute's silence was interrupted after which the Chairman carried out the ceremony next to the players' tunnel. The plaque was later relocated to the north east corner of the stadium, close to the scene of the 1971 accident. A brief inscription below the Rangers crest stated, simply, *In memory of all those who died as a result of the disaster at Ibrox Stadium on 2nd January 1971.* Not until the 30th anniversary though, would Rangers fans see construction of a larger and more fitting memorial to those who had perished on Stairway 13.

The event on the afternoon of Tuesday 2 January 2001 had for many, been a long time in coming. While the re-built Ibrox Stadium, Rangers declared, stood as testament to those who had lost their lives in the disaster, many fans and relatives of the deceased had yearned for the erection of a more personal memorial. The mood was sombre and the weather dull and damp as former Rangers players, officials, supporters and official dignitaries gathered at the south east corner of the Rangers stadium. The occasion was a 3.00pm religious service to remember the tragic events of 30 years earlier, coupled with the unveiling of a statue to mark the blackest day in Rangers' 108-year history. Four hundred and seventy one relatives of those who had perished on that fateful day were in attendance as were the then current Rangers and Celtic chairmen, David Murray and Brian Quinn. Former Rangers players John Greig, Sandy Jardine, Derek Johnstone, Willie Henderson and the then manager, Dick Advocaat, were all in attendance, as were Celtic's representatives, Billy McNeill and Sean Fallon. Environment Minister, Sam Galbraith, Glasgow Lord Provost, Alex Mosson, Glasgow Chief Constable, John Orr and members of the emergency services were also present. Inside the stadium, 5,000 people were seated to watch a relay of the proceedings shown on the large screen that is situated in the north east corner of the ground.

The 20-minute service, which incorporated a one minute silence and a prayer of dedication, was led by long-time Rangers supporter, Reverend Stuart McQuarrie. He commenced, 'On behalf of the chairman and directors of Rangers Football Club, may I welcome each and every one of you to this special memorial service. During this service, we will commemorate the lives of those who died in the tragic accident here at Ibrox Stadium on 2 January 1971. Today it is the families and relatives who are the special guests of Rangers Football Club.' He added, 'Many of us share a passion for Rangers, including some like me who were at that game and others who are here with us following the service within the stadium wanting to pay their own tribute. The focal point of today's service is the families and relatives of those whose lives were lost. Each life represents a particular and unique tragedy for which many people have lived with its consequences.' During the service, Chairman David Murray unveiled the memorial. It revealed a bronze statue of Rangers former stalwart, John Greig with his head turned slightly and a football held in his left hand resting nonchalantly against his side. Below the statue, two blue embossed plaques were revealed detailing the names of each of the 66 victims of the 1971 disaster as well as those who had lost their lives in the earlier tragedies of 1902 and 1961. Relatives of the victims of 1971 laid wreaths at the base of the memorial. Some of those in attendance were visibly emotional in what was a most sombre occasion. David Murray later commented, 'I was pleased to see so many supporters turn out. It was a day in which to put everything into perspective. We have acknowledged for some time that something like this needs to be done. This was about the families and we are simply speaking on their behalf.'[1]

While the service was taking place at Ibrox, more than 59,000 supporters obeyed a one-minute silence at Celtic Park before Celtic's game against Kilmarnock. Similar silences were observed at football grounds throughout Scotland. Rangers themselves did not play until the evening of that day, where they faced an away fixture against St Mirren. Perhaps there was greater significance for the 22 players and 8,142 spectators who stood to observe the minute's silence before their match commenced that night. Three decades had elapsed since that January day in 1971 and yet the passing of time had failed to dim the crystal clear memories of that terrible day in Govan. The enduring sadness remains that 66 Rangers supporters left their homes on that bleak, bitterly cold January day to support their football team, yet fate would dictate that they would never return to the warmth of their loved ones.

CHAPTER ELEVEN

SET IN STONE

Andy Scott of 'Scott Associates, Sculpture & Design (Glasgow)' was awarded the commission to create a fitting tribute to those who died.

I have to admit my own personal memories of the disaster at the Stadium are hazy. I was only five at the time. My father was at the game and did what he could, along with many others, to help at the scene. I remember he was very late coming home that night and I remember my mother's concern and subsequent relief on his return. As a five-year-old you're kind of oblivious to the tragedies of others in the world of grown-ups. I don't remember my father going to many games afterwards.

It never dissuaded his interest in football though and I grew up with tales of 'Baxter's Wembley' and marvelled like all wee boys at the exploits of the players of the Old Firm, the Scotland national team and the big names of the English and European game.

Rangers were a constant presence as I grew up attending nearby Bellahouston Academy and, in recent years, I've rediscovered my passion for the team. Working seven days a week as a professional sculptor rarely allows me the time to go to games, though I revel in the occasional midweek games which I can get to. So being awarded the commission to create a memorial to the disaster was a very proud moment as an artist and as a Rangers fan.

After presenting a couple of ideas to the Club, the figure of John Greig was chosen. He was the captain of the team on that fateful day in 1971 and had recently been voted the greatest ever Rangers player. I was very aware, however, of the challenge in the subject matter.

This was not to be simply a statue of the man but would be an emblem of respect, a figure of contemplation and remembrance for those who had lost their lives and as the artist responsible, I would have to be conscious of all these implications.

On the technical and logistic side of things it was a complicated commission, which the public would be largely unaware of. Considerations such as the location, the foundation, the brickwork plinth and the plaques all took careful and intricate planning.

Many people were involved in the process and should be credited for their role in making the memorial happen. Staff of the club of course and the contractors but a special role was undertaken by Senga Murray, who is a painter and is responsible for the superb range of portraits in The Blue Room and elsewhere in Ibrox. She assumed the role of project co-ordinator and helped greatly in managing the commission, allowing me to get on with the very challenging task of actually sculpting the statue.

Various technical considerations had to be dealt with. Were the foundations already in place for the stairwell on Edmiston Drive in the right place and would they take the weight of the statue and plinth? Could we source Imperial size red facing bricks, which the Planning Department asked for to match the existing stadium façade? When would there be a window of opportunity between games to allow the plinth to be built and the sculpture to be installed? What would the optimum position be to allow unimpeded flow of crowds around the statue on match days and maintain the maximum visual impact the memorial deserved?

Over a series of meetings all these issues and others were resolved and meanwhile, at my studio on the other side of Glasgow, the statue took shape. With the very tight schedule to meet the unveiling date, I enlisted the assistance of Alison Bell, a friend and established portrait artist who worked with me on the clay modelling of the statue. Her help was invaluable in working at the speed and precision which was required in this instance.

We worked from numerous photos of John Greig to compose his likeness in clay over a welded steel internal frame and it was a moment of great relief and pride when Mr Greig himself came to the studio with his wife to approve the likeness. Finally, the statue was cast into bronze and delivered to site and installed.

And there it stands today as a poignant tribute to those who didn't come home from the match that day and indeed from the other tragic events at the stadium in 1961 and 1902.

The figure stands in contemplative stillness, posed as though pausing in a moment's silence. He wears an armband of respect and looks round in the direction of Stairway 13 where the tragedy unfolded.

The unveiling was one of the proudest moments of my professional life. When you make a piece of sculpture, you get caught up in the physical process and intricacies of the job and, in a sense, become removed from the purpose. When it was finally unveiled in front of thousands of people (including my own father) who had turned up to see it, remember and pay their respects, I was overwhelmed. The intensity of the occasion reached a peak for me that night though and the emotion hit home when it was the opening item on the national television news. A packed Celtic Park stood for a minute's silence. Given the rivalry between the clubs, which often transcends commonsense, this mark of respect was especially poignant.

It is not often that you're lucky enough to combine the great passions of your life and to be able to do so for such an emotive purpose is all the more challenging and rewarding. It is a unique emotion to stand amongst the crowd outside the stadium before or after a match and hear and see the reactions of the fans. I'm just another fan amongst the thousands there but to have physically crafted the sculpture which they pause to admire makes it a very humbling experience.

I can only hope that my efforts are appreciated by the bereaved because ultimately, it is their statue as much as the club's.

At the time of writing I've started work on the memorial statue to Jim Baxter and I'm lucky that my job as a sculptor brings about a great deal of interesting and rewarding commissions. I doubt however, that many will match the emotional intensity and the honour of creating the Ibrox Disaster Memorial.

CHAPTER TWELVE

PLAYER BIOGRAPHIES 1970/71

TOM ALEXANDER

Born in Ayr, 20 October 1951. Alexander joined Rangers in July 1970 and made his debut at right back in the away league game against Cowdenbeath in April 1971 where he played in Sandy Jardine's normal position. He kept his place for the next league game against St Johnstone at home but his two appearances proved to be the beginning and the end of his first team career at Ibrox.

ALFIE CONN

Born in Edinburgh, 5 April 1952. Played in schools football before being rejected by Leeds United, Conn joined Rangers in October 1968 and made his debut in the next month in the away leg of the European Fairs Cup 2nd round tie against Dundalk. A skilful midfield player, Conn, due to injuries, never managed to fully establish himself in the Rangers first team though he won a Scottish League Cup winners medal in 1970/71, a Scottish Cup winners medal in 1973 and was a part of the successful 1972 European Cup Winners Cup team which triumphed in Barcelona. Having scored 23 league goals for Rangers in 77 appearances, Conn was transferred to Tottenham Hotspur in July 1974 where he scored six league goals in 35 starts for the north London Club. He returned to Glasgow in March 1977 to play for Celtic and scored eight goals in 34 games. In March 1979 Conn played and scored in his last game for Celtic before he was released. Brief spells with Derby County, Hercules Alicante in America followed before Conn returned to Scotland in August 1980 to play for Hearts. After scoring three league goals in 13 starts at Tynecastle, Conn joined Blackpool in March 1981 where he played three league games. His contract was cancelled the following month and he returned once again to Scotland in August 1981 to play for Motherwell, managing three league goals in 21 games before his last match at Fir Park in October 1982. Conn won two Scotland caps in 1975 whilst at Tottenham Hotspur and more may have followed had his team been more successful at that time.

JIM DENNY

Born in Paisley, 13 March 1950. Denny joined Rangers in January 1971 to amazingly make his debut in the Scottish Cup final in May that year where he played at right back in the narrow defeat by Celtic. Although a useful squad player who was capable of playing in any position for Rangers, Denny's opportunities were limited at Ibrox and he managed just 30 league appearances in eight seasons for Rangers. He was transferred to Hearts in September 1979 and played 38 times in the league during that season. He made a further 19 league appearances for Hearts the following season before joining Stirling Albion where he made 20 league appearances during the 1981/82 season. Whilst Denny was unable to make a regular place his own at Rangers, his loyalty to the club was admirable considering his limited opportunities.

GRAHAM FYFE

Born in Motherwell, 18 August 1951. Fyfe joined Rangers in December 1968 and made his debut in March 1970 in the home league game against Hearts. Never more than a bit part player, Fyfe was a roving forward who scored 22 league goals in 41 appearances over seven seasons. Although a valuable member of the squad, he was unlucky not to win a medal during his time at Ibrox. He was transferred to Hibernian yet played only nine league games for them, scoring once before joining Dumbarton in the summer of 1978. Fyfe scored four league goals in 28 appearances in his first season and followed this up with seven league goals in 25 appearances in 1978/79 before his departure. He was unlucky perhaps, to have been part of a Rangers squad which contained forwards of the quality of Stein, Johnston, Johnstone, Henderson and Parlane otherwise he would surely have figured more frequently in first team action.

JOHN GREIG

Born in Edinburgh, 11 September 1942. Previously with Edina Hearts, Greig joined Rangers in August 1960 and made a scoring debut in the home Scottish League Cup tie against Airdrie. A Rangers player for 18 years, Greig was ultimately voted by the club's supporters as the 'Greatest Ever Ranger' in 2000. He won 16 medals during his career at Ibrox and his finest hour was probably captaining his team to the 1972 European Cup Winners Cup success. Though he originally performed as a forward, Greig was moved back to defensive duties, where he effectively marshalled the Rangers back line throughout the sixties and seventies. He helped achieve a treble in 1963/64 and repeated the feat in 1975/76 and again in 1977/78. A wonderful servant to Rangers, he scored 87 league goals in 495 appearances. He announced his retirement in May 1978 at the age of 35 and was immediately appointed Rangers manager when Jock Wallace announced his decision to move to Leicester City. Under Greig's guidance Rangers won the Scottish Cup in 1979 and the Scottish League Cup in 1978/79 and 1981/82 though league success remained sadly elusive. With his team struggling to find consistency, Greig resigned as manager in October 1983, though he later returned to the Club to serve firstly as a public relations manager and later as a Director. Greig captained Scotland 15 times in 44 appearances and scored three goals but arguably it is his magnificent contribution to his club which is most fondly remembered by the Rangers support.

WILLIE HENDERSON

Born in Baillieston, 24 January 1944. Formerly playing in Airdrie schools football, Henderson joined Rangers in August 1960 and made his debut in the home league game against Clyde in March 1961. Though small in stature, the 'Wee Barra' combined speed and trickery to bamboozle opposition defences and became a firm favourite with the Rangers fans. The right winger bagged eight medals whilst with Rangers, although he failed to make the team for the 1972 European Cup Winners Cup final for what proved to be Rangers finest hour. In July 1972, after scoring 35 league goals in 274 appearances, the diminutive forward moved to Sheffield Wednesday where he played 42 games over two seasons for the 'Owls' before departing for Hong Kong Rangers. Henderson returned to Scottish football to play one full league game for Airdrie in October 1978 before retiring at the end of the 1978/79 season. Known for wearing contact lenses on the playing field, Henderson gained 29 caps for Scotland, all achieved whilst playing for Rangers.

COLIN JACKSON

Born in London, 8 October 1946. Jackson joined Rangers in October 1963 after appearing for Sunnybank Athletic in Aberdeen and made his debut in January 1966 in the home league game against Partick Thistle. Initially only a bit part player at Ibrox during the 1960s, Jackson forced his way into the Rangers first team in 1970/71 and became a consistent performer in defence for the next 12 seasons. He won Scottish Championship medals in 1974/75, 1975/76 and 1977/78 together with Scottish Cup winners medals in 1976, 1978 and 1979 as well as Scottish League Cup winners medals in 1970/71, 1975/76, 1977/78, 1978/79 and 1981/82. Jackson played in 339 league games for Rangers and scored 23 goals before he was transferred to Morton for the start of the 1982/83 season. At Cappielow he made five league appearances under the guidance of his old team-mate Alex Miller before a further switch to Partick Thistle, though he failed to make a first team appearance for the Firhill Club. A solid performer with Rangers who won eight caps for Scotland (all whilst at Rangers), scoring one goal.

SANDY JARDINE

Born in Edinburgh, 31 December 1948. Formerly a product of Edinburgh schools football, Jardine joined Rangers in December 1965 and made his debut in February 1967 against Hearts in a home league game. Jardine won Scottish Championship medals at Ibrox in 1974/75, 1975/76 and 1977/78 and Scottish FA Cup winners medals in 1973, 1976, 1978, 1979 and 1981. He also won Scottish League Cup winners medals 1970/71, 1975/76, 1977/78, 1978/79 and 1981/82 as well as a European Cup Winners Cup medal in 1972. Although Jardine played his formative years in a variety of positions, he established himself as a consistent and reliable full-back who gave Rangers 16 seasons loyal service before his departure in May 1982 at the age of 33. He scored 42 league goals in 431 appearances for Rangers before moving back to his native city to join Hearts in July 1982. Jardine proved a revelation at Tynecastle by continuing to play on for a further six seasons.

He scored three league goals in 184 games for Hearts, missing only 16 league games in his first five seasons. Whilst playing at Tynecastle, Jardine also held the position of co-manager with his former Rangers team-mate, Alex MacDonald who also continued to play into the 1985/86 season. Jardine left his position with Hearts in 1988 to pursue a career in business. He has since returned to Ibrox to work for the club's commercial department. Capped 38 times for Scotland (all won whilst at Rangers) scoring once, Jardine ranks amongst Rangers' best ever full-backs.

WILLIE JOHNSTON

Born in Glasgow, 19 December 1946. Formerly with Lochore Welfare, Johnston nicknamed 'Bud', joined Rangers in April 1964 and made his debut against St Johnstone in the home Scottish League Cup tie in August 1964. An exciting and speedy left winger, Johnston, unfairly perhaps, became as well known for his fiery temper as for his playing ability. Though sent off six times in his formative years at Ibrox, Johnston gained four major medals during an eight-year stint at Rangers. His finest moment was probably scoring two goals in the European Cup Winners Cup success against Moscow Dynamo. Having made 209 league appearances for Rangers, he was transferred to West Bromwich Albion in December 1972 where he played 203 league games for the Midlands Club. Sandwiched between his career in Britain, Johnston spent three seasons (1979, 1980 and 1982) playing for Vancouver Whitecaps in the North American Soccer League. In October 1979, he moved to Birmingham City and made 15 league appearances before rejoining Rangers in August 1980. Beyond 34 years of age, Johnston played 27 more league games at Ibrox before a further move in September 1982 saw him take up the position of player-coach at Hearts where he played 30 league games. A final switch in April 1985 saw Johnston play three games for East Fife in a further role as player-coach before retirement beckoned. Capped 22 times for Scotland (nine won whilst at Rangers) Johnston gained unwanted notoriety when he was sent home from the 1978 World Cup Finals for testing positive for illegal stimulants. Such commotion and the 16 sending offs he received during his 20 year playing career possibly masks the exciting and skilful ability he possessed.

Derek Johnstone

Born in Dundee, 4 November 1953. Signed from Dundee schools football in July 1970, Johnstone made his debut at the age of 16 in September 1970 in the home league game against Cowdenbeath and marked the occasion by scoring two goals. Johnstone amassed a haul of 14 medals at Ibrox and achieved the incredible feat of scoring the only goal in the Scottish League Cup final victory against Celtic in October 1970. Equally at home as a forward or in the centre of defence, Johnstone performed admirably in the latter position in the 1972 European Cup Winners Cup victory when still only 18. Johnstone though, proved a prolific marksman, scoring 129 league goals in 340 games including 25 league goals in 33 games during the 1977/78 treble winning season. He was transferred to Chelsea in September 1983 yet made only one full league appearance in two seasons for the west London side. During the 1983/84, season 'DJ' was loaned to Dundee United and made two full league appearances, though he failed to score. In January 1985, Johnstone returned to play for Rangers although it proved to be an unsuccessful spell and he managed to score only one league goal in 19 appearances before his departure in June 1986. A further four league appearances followed when Johnstone played for Partick Thistle during the 1986/87 season before he later briefly, managed the Firhill Club. He won all 14 of his Scotland caps whilst at Rangers, scoring two goals, though it is his goal scoring display during his first spell at Ibrox which fans remember most fondly.

Alex MacDonald

Born in Glasgow, 17 March 1948. Previously with Luncarty Juniors, MacDonald signed for Rangers from St Johnstone in November 1968 where he had made 64 league appearances. He made his Rangers debut in the same month in the away league match at Clyde. Nicknamed 'Doddie' by the Rangers faithful, MacDonald won 12 medals during his Rangers career including an appearance in the 1972 European Cup Winners Cup success. A loyal and dedicated servant to Rangers, MacDonald proved an industrious left sided midfield player where he became a mainstay throughout the seventies. He was transferred to Hearts in July 1980 and then became player and co-manager the following season. MacDonald scored 12 goals for Hearts in 105 league appearances, making a final brief substitute appearance in

September 1985 before retiring as a player. Sacked as manager of Hearts in September 1990, he became manager of Airdrie and led them to the Scottish Cup finals of 1992 and 1995. A winner of a single Scotland cap during his time at Rangers, MacDonald is remembered as a key member of the Ibrox team which clinched the treble in 1975/76 and 1977/78.

ANGUS MCCALLUM

Born in Glasgow, 19 March 1953. McCallum joined Rangers in May 1970 and made his debut and sole first team appearance at centre half for Rangers in the home league game against St Mirren on Boxing Day 1970. Unable to force his way into the first team, McCallum was released by Rangers at the end of the 1970/71 season.

PETER MCCLOY

Born in Girvan, 26 November 1946. Signed from Motherwell in March 1970 where he had made 137 league appearances, McCloy made his Rangers debut in the same month in the away league game against Dunfermline Athletic. Known as the 'Girvan Lighthouse', McCloy won 11 medals at Ibrox including the success against Moscow Dynamo. His career at Rangers looked in jeopardy after the arrival of Stewart Kennedy towards the end of the 1972/73 season although it was not until the 1974/75 season that Kennedy replaced McCloy completely. Despite not playing a single league game during that season and largely playing a supporting role to Kennedy for the next three seasons, McCloy eventually made the goalkeepers shirt his own once more as Kennedy moved on to Forfar Athletic. McCloy played in 350 league games for Rangers before announcing his retirement in August 1986, just three months short of his 40th birthday. He won four caps for Scotland, which were all achieved during his time at Rangers and may well have made more appearances for his country but for strong competition for the goalkeeper's jersey during his lengthy playing career.

Iain McDonald

Born in Edinburgh, 26 November 1946. McDonald joined Rangers in September 1969 and made his debut in January 1970 in the home league game against Ayr United. McDonald was an outside left who played in the shadow of Willie Johnston though he scored two league goals in 11 appearances. He received a serious injury whilst at Ibrox and he was told he would never play again but he made a miraculous recovery and moved on to join Dundee United where he scored six league goals in 26 appearances at Tannadice before playing his last game in December 1975.

Ronnie McKinnon

Born in Glasgow, 20 August 1940. McKinnon joined Rangers in July 1958 from Dunipace Juniors and made his debut in March 1961 in the home league game against Hearts. McKinnon won Scottish Championship medals in 1962/63 and 1963/64 and Scottish Cup winners medals in 1962, 1963, 1964 and 1966. In addition he won Scottish League Cup winners medals in 1963/64, 1964/65 and 1970/71. Tragically, he broke his leg in the European Cup Winners Cup 2nd round 2nd leg tie against Sporting Lisbon in November 1971 and missed out on the final success in Barcelona. The injury effectively finished McKinnon's career and he was released at the end of the 1972/73 season. Capped 28 times for Scotland, scoring once, the commanding centre half will always be remembered as part of the formidable half back line of Greig, McKinnon and Baxter.

Willie Mathieson

Born in St Andrews, 20 January 1943. Mathieson joined Rangers from St Andrews United in August 1963 and made his debut in February 1965 in the home Scottish Cup tie against Hamilton Academical. Dubbed 'Willie Wan Fit' by the Rangers faithful, Mathieson was unable to gain a regular first team place at Ibrox until the 1967/68 season. A solid left back, Mathieson scored two league goals for Rangers in 175 appearances before later switching to Raith Rovers, where he played in 13 league games during the early part of the 1976/77 season.

ALEX MILLER

Born in Glasgow, 4 July 1949. Miller joined Rangers in April 1967 from Clydebank Juniors and made his debut in the home Scottish League Cup tie against Morton in August 1970. A competent full back for Rangers, Miller won Scottish Championship medals in 1974/75, 1975/76 and 1977/78 and Scottish Cup winners medals in 1976 and 1979. Additionally, he helped Rangers to Scottish League Cup success in 1970/71, 1977/78, 1978/79 and 1981/82. After scoring 17 league goals in 159 appearances, he left Rangers to play the 1982/83 season in South China though he returned to Scotland to take charge of Morton for the start of the 1983/84 season, where he played in the first eight league games, scoring once. Miller then surprisingly quit both playing and managing at Cappielow to take up the manager's chair at St Mirren. He then left Love Street to take the reins at Hibernian early in the 1986/87 season. He quit once again in the autumn of the 1996 season to become assistant manager to Gordon Strachan at Coventry City, a role he also held with the Scotland national team under Craig Brown. Miller returned to Scotland again in January 1998 to manage Aberdeen, though his spell at Pittodrie proved unsuccessful and he was sacked barely 12 months later. In September 1999, he became Chief Scout at Liverpool before promotion to first team coach. Though a solid performer during his days at Ibrox, Miller is arguably better remembered for his career since he finished playing.

GERRY NEEF

Born in Hausham, Upper Bavaria, 30 December 1946. Neef joined Rangers in August 1968 and made his debut in April 1969 in the league game against Morton. An agile goalkeeper, Neef became the first German to play for Rangers and turned out in 33 league games before playing his last match in the away league game against Arbroath in October 1972.

DEREK PARLANE

Born in Helensburgh, 5 May 1953. Initially on the books of Queens Park without making an appearance for the 'Spiders', Parlane joined Rangers in April 1970 and made his debut in the home league game against St Mirren on Boxing Day, 1970. It was not until the 1972/73 season though, that he became a first team regular. Parlane became an integral part of the Scottish Championship winning side of 1974/75 and of the Scottish Premier Division Champions in 1975/76 and 1977/78. He also won Scottish Cup winners medals in 1975/76, 1977/78 and 1978/79. After scoring 80 league goals in 168 full appearances for Rangers, Parlane was transferred to Leeds United in March 1980 where he scored ten league goals in 45 appearances before a loan spell in Hong Kong. He returned to Britain to secure a transfer to Manchester City, in August 1983, where he scored a further 20 league goals in 47 appearances. Parlane was transferred to Swansea City in January 1985 (three league goals in 21 appearances) before switching to Racing Jet in Belgium. In December 1986, he was transferred to Rochdale where he scored ten goals in 42 appearances before returning to Scotland in December 1987 to join Airdrie, where he finished his career by scoring four league goals in nine appearances. Parlane remained a consistent scorer during his career although he managed to secure only one goal for Scotland in his 12 appearances (all whilst at Rangers).

ANDY PENMAN

Born in Rosyth, 20 February 1943. Penman joined Rangers in April 1967 from Dundee with whom he won a Scottish League winners medal and a sole Scotland cap. He made his debut for Rangers in the away Scottish League Cup tie against Aberdeen in August 1967 and scored eight league goals in 24 appearances in his first season for the club. A classy midfield player, Penman notched 15 league goals in 26 appearances the following season with only Willie Johnston scoring more goals. His consistency continued as he netted ten league goals in 25 appearances in 1969/70 before his first team opportunities became more limited and he played his last game for the Club in the home Scottish League Cup fixture against St Mirren in August 1972. Penman scored 36 league goals in 88 appearances for Rangers before being transferred to Arbroath during the 1972/73 season. His goal return failed to be as good for the 'Red Lichties', as he scored only ten league goals in 75 appearances in four seasons. Penman joined Inverness Caley in 1976 and retired three years later. Rangers fans were saddened to hear of his untimely death in July 1994 at the age of 51.

BILLY SEMPLE

Born in Bellshill, 2 November 1946. Semple joined Rangers in 1967 and made his debut for the Club in January 1968 in the home league game against Partick Thistle. An outside left, Semple made eight league appearances for Rangers, scoring twice before being given a free transfer in May 1972.

DAVE SMITH

Born in Aberdeen, 14 November 1943. Smith joined Rangers in August 1966 from Aberdeen and made his debut in the same month against Hibernian in the home Scottish League Cup tie. A classy left half, Smith won only a European Cup Winners Cup medal in 1972 during his Rangers career. After scoring eight league goals in 187 games, he joined Arbroath in November 1974 to become player/coach where he played 20 league games without scoring. Smith was reunited with former team-mate Andy Penman for the 1974/75 season, though it proved something of a disaster as Arbroath finished bottom of the league. In May 1976, Smith played five games for Seattle Sounders before joining Los Angeles Aztecs in June of the same year, where he played 16 times. In October 1976, Smith became player/manager of Berwick Rangers where he scored nine league goals in 146 appearances before later managing Peterhead. Capped twice for Scotland, once whilst with Rangers in 1968, Smith is fondly remembered by those who saw him as a stylish performer.

COLIN STEIN

Born in Philipstoun, 10 May 1947, Stein played for both Broxburn Strollers and Armadale Thistle before making his league debut for Hibernian in 1965/66. After scoring 41 league goals in 70 appearances for the Edinburgh side, he was transferred to Rangers for a then record fee of £100,000 in October 1968. He made his debut in the away league game against Arbroath in November that year, scoring a hat-trick, a feat he repeated the following week against his former club at Ibrox. Stein became a big favourite with the Rangers following and secured six medals including the European triumph in 1972. Despite scoring 60 league goals in 111 starts for Rangers, he was transferred to Coventry City in October 1972 where he managed 22 league goals in 83 appearances. The prolific centre forward was then transferred back to Rangers in March 1975 where his first team opportunities were limited. He managed to score four league goals in 23 appearances during his second spell at Ibrox before joining Kilmarnock on loan in October 1977. During his only season at Rugby Park, Stein scored eight league goals in 23 appearances. Surprisingly perhaps, after being offered a free transfer by Rangers he elected instead to retire and left the game prematurely at the age of 31. Capped 17 times for Scotland, all of which he won during his time at Ibrox, he scored ten goals. Coupled to the 97 goals in 206 appearances Stein scored for Rangers, highlights his prolific goal return.

BOBBY WATSON

Born in Glasgow, 22 March 1950. Watson joined Rangers in July 1970 from Ardrossan Winton Rovers and made his debut in goal in the home Scottish League Cup match against Dunfermline Athletic the following month. After playing in the Glasgow Cup final against Celtic two days later, he conceded three goals and was never chosen to represent Rangers in the first team again. He departed Ibrox at the end of the 1972/73 season.

KENNY WATSON

Born in Edinburgh, 1952, Watson joined Rangers in November 1968 and made his debut in December 1969 in the home league game against Clyde, replacing Jim Baxter. A left sided midfield player, Watson made three league appearances for Rangers before being released at the end of the 1970/71 season.

Notes

PREFACE
[1] Display, National Football Museum, Preston, 21 March 2001.
[2] Ibid
[3] Ibid
[4] Ibid

CHAPTER FIVE – AFTERMATH
[1] Glasgow Herald, 4 January 1971.
[2] Ibid.
[3] Scottish Daily Express, 4 January 1971.
[4] Ibid.
[5] Ibid.
[6] Glasgow Herald, 4 January 1971.
[7] Glasgow Herald, 5 January 1971.
[8] Ibid.
[9] Ibid.
[10] Ibid.
[11] Scottish Daily Express, 4 January 1971.
[12] Ibid.
[13] Ibid.
[14] Ibid.
[15] Daily Record, 5 January 1971.
[16] Ibid.
[17] Ibid.
[18] Ibid.
[19] Glasgow Herald, 4 January 1971.
[20] London Times, 4 January 1971.

CHAPTER SIX – TORNADO OF GRIEF
[1] Glasgow Herald, 5 January 1971.
[2] Scottish Daily Express, 4 January,1971.
[3] Glasgow Herald, 6 January 1971.
[4] Daily Record, 1 January 2001.

CHAPTER SEVEN – OLD FIRM UNITED
[1] Scotland XI versus Rangers/Celtic Select, match programme, 27 January 1971.
[2] Glasgow Herald, 27 January, 1971.
[3] Scotland XI versus Rangers/Celtic Select, match programme, 27 January 1971.

CHAPTER EIGHT – THE INQUIRY
[1] Glasgow Herald, 17 February 1971.
[2] Ibid
[3] Ibid
[4] Glasgow Herald, 18 February 1971.
[5] Glasgow Herald, 19 February 1971.
[6] Ibid
[7] Ibid
[8] Glasgow Herald, 23 February 1971.
[9] Glasgow Herald, 24 February 1971
[10] Glasgow Herald, 24 October 1974.
[11] Ibid.

CHAPTER NINE – 'DEEDLE'
[1] The London Times, 4 January 1971.
[2] Evening Times (Glasgow), 14 October 1992.

CHAPTER TEN – IN MEMORIAM
[1] Evening Times, (Glasgow), 3 January 2001.

APPENDIX 1

Rangers Playing Record 1970/71

Scottish League Division 1

29 August
V St Mirren (Away) 0-0
McCloy, Jardine, Miller, Greig, McKinnon, Jackson, Fyfe, Conn, Stein, MacDonald A., Johnston. **Attendance: 27,400**

5 September
V Falkirk (Home) 2-0
McCloy, Jardine, Miller, Greig, McKinnon, Jackson, Fyfe, Conn, Stein, MacDonald A., Johnston (2 (1 pen)). **Attendance: 39,000**

12 September
V Celtic (Away) 0-2
McCloy, Jardine, Miller, Greig, McKinnon, Jackson, Fyfe (Penman), MacDonald A., Stein, Johnston, Conn. **Attendance: 75,000**

19 September
V Cowdenbeath (Home) 5-0
McCloy, Jardine, Miller, Greig (2), McKinnon, Jackson, Henderson, Conn, Johnstone (2), MacDonald A. (1), Fyfe.
Attendance: 31,000

26 September
V Dundee United (Away) 2-0
McCloy, Jardine, Miller, Greig, McKinnon, Jackson, Fyfe (1), Conn (1), Stein, MacDonald A., Johnston.
Attendance: 23,000

3 October
V Motherwell (Home) 3-1
McCloy, Jardine, Miller, Conn, McKinnon, Jackson, Henderson, Fyfe, Stein (1) (Johnstone), MacDonald A. (1), Johnston (1).
Attendance: 37,000

10 October
V Hearts (Away) 1-0
McCloy, Jardine, Miller, Greig, McKinnon, Jackson, Henderson, Conn (Fyfe), Stein, MacDonald A., Johnston (1 pen).
Attendance: 32,500

17 October
V Aberdeen (Home) 0-2
McCloy, Jardine, Miller, Greig, McKinnon, Jackson, Henderson, Fyfe, Stein, MacDonald A. (Smith), Johnston.
Attendance: 39,763

31 October
V Airdrie (Home) 5-0
McCloy, Jardine, Miller, Conn (1), McKinnon, Jackson, Henderson, MacDonald A., Johnstone, Stein (2), Johnston (2 (1 pen)).
Attendance: 28,788

7 November
V Dunferline Athletic (Away) 1-1
McCloy, Jardine, Miller, Greig (MacDonald A.), McKinnon, Jackson (1), Henderson, Conn, Johnstone, Stein, Johnston.
Attendance: 20,000

14 November
V Clyde (Home) 5-0
Mulherron (og).
McCloy, Jardine, Miller, Conn (Fyfe), McKinnon, Jackson, Henderson, MacDonald A., Johnstone (1), Stein (2), Johnston (1 pen).
Attendance: 25,915

21 November
V Ayr United (Away) 1-2 Young (og).
McCloy, Jardine, Miller, Conn (Johnstone), McKinnon, Jackson, Henderson, MacDonald A., Stein, Fyfe, Johnston.
Attendance: 20,000

25 November
V Hibernian (Away) 2-3
McCloy, Jardine, Miller, Conn, McKinnon, Jackson, Henderson (Smith), MacDonald A., Johnstone (1), Stein (1), Fyfe.
Attendance: 18,770

28 November
V Morton (Away) 2-1
McCloy, Jardine, Miller, Conn (1), McKinnon, Jackson, Henderson, MacDonald A., Johnstone (Fyfe (1)), Stein, Johnston. **Attendance: 15,000**

5 December
V Dundee (Home) 0-0
McCloy, Jardine, Miller, Greig, McKinnon, Jackson, Henderson, Conn, Stein, Fyfe, MacDonald A. **Attendance: 25,420**

12 December
V St Johnstone (Away) 1-2
McCloy, Jardine, Miller, Greig, McKinnon, Jackson, Henderson, Conn (Johnstone), Stein, Fyfe (1), MacDonald A.
Attendance: 10,500

19 December
V Kilmarnock (Home) 4-2
McCloy, Jardine, Miller, Greig, McKinnon, Jackson (1), Henderson, Stein, Johnstone (2), Smith, MacDonald A (1).
Attendance: 19,450

26 December
V St Mirren (Home) 1-0
McCloy, Jardine, Miller, Greig (1), McCallum, Jackson, Fyfe, Parlane, Johnstone, MacDonald A., Semple.
Attendance: 25,000

1 January
V Falkirk (Away) 1-3
Neef, Jardine, Mathieson, Greig, McKinnon, Jackson, Henderson (MacDonald A.), Conn (1), Johnstone, Smith, Stein. **Attendance: 18,000**

2 January
V Celtic (Home) 1-1
Neef, Jardine, Mathieson, Greig, McKinnon, Jackson, Henderson (MacDonald A.), Conn, Johnstone, Smith, Stein (1). **Attendance: 80,057**

16 January
V Dundee United (Home) 1-1
Neef, Jardine, Mathieson (MacDonald A.), Greig (1), McKinnon, Jackson, Henderson, Conn, Stein, Smith Johnston.
Attendance: 27,776

30 January
V Motherwell (Away) 2-1
McCloy, Jardine, Mathieson (1), Greig, McKinnon, Jackson, Henderson, Conn (MacDonald A.), Stein (1), Smith, Johnston.
Attendance: 22,500

6 February
V Hearts (Home) 1-0
McCloy, Jardine, Mathieson, Greig, McKinnon, Jackson, Henderson (1), MacDonald A., Johnstone (Conn), Smith, Johnston. **Attendance: 29,398**

20 February
V Aberdeen (Away) 0-0
McCloy, Jardine, Mathieson, Greig, McKinnon, Jackson, Henderson, Conn, Stein, MacDonald A. (Johnstone), Johnston.
Attendance: 36,000

27 February
V Hibernian (Home) 1-1
McCloy, Jardine, Mathieson, Greig (1), Jackson, Watson K., Henderson, MacDonald A., Stein, Smith, McDonald I. (Parlane). **Attendance: 30,644**

10 March
V Airdrie (Away) 3-4
McCloy, Jardine, Mathieson, Greig,
McKinnon, Jackson, Henderson,
MacDonald A. (2), Stein (1), Smith
(Parlane), Johnston. **Attendance: 15,000**

13 March
V Dunfermline Athletic (Home) 2-0
McCloy, Jardine, Mathieson, Greig (1),
McKinnon, Jackson, Henderson (1),
MacDonald A., Stein, Johnston,
McDonald I. **Attendance: 21,580**

20 March
V Clyde (Away) 2-2
McCloy, Jardine, Mathieson, Greig,
McKinnon, Jackson, Henderson,
MacDonald A. (Penman), Stein (1), Conn,
Johnston (1). **Attendance: 10,500**

27 March
V Ayr United (Home) 2-0
McCloy, Jardine, Miller, Greig (1),
McKinnon, Jackson, Henderson, Penman,
Parlane, Johnston (1), McDonald I.
(MacDonald A). **Attendance: 22,000**

3 April
V Morton (Home) 0-0
McCloy, Jardine, Mathieson, Greig,
McKinnon, Jackson, Henderson, Penman
(Conn), Stein, Johnstone, Johnston.
Attendance: 13,986

10 April
V Dundee (Away) 0-1
McCloy, Miller, Mathieson, Jardine
(Penman), McKinnon, Jackson, Henderson,
MacDonald A., Stein, Greig, Johnston.
Attendance: 18,000

14 April
V Cowdenbeath (Away) 3-1
McCloy, Alexander, Mathieson, Jardine (1)
(Penman), McKinnon, Jackson, Henderson,
MacDonald A., Stein (1), Greig (1),
Johnston.
Attendance: 3,396

17 April
V St Johnstone (Home) 0-2
McCloy, Alexander, Mathieson, Greig,
McKinnon, Jackson, Henderson, Penman,
Stein, MacDonald A., Johnston.
Attendance: 17,566

24 April
V Kilmarnock (Away) 4-1
McCloy, Jardine, Miller (1), Conn,
McKinnon, Jackson, Henderson (1),
MacDonald A. (1), Johnstone, Stein (1),
Johnston. **Attendance: 8,544**

EUROPEAN FAIRS CUP

16 September, 1st Round, 1st Leg
V Bayern Munich (Away) 0-1
McCloy, Jardine, Miller, Greig, McKinnon,
Jackson, Fyfe, Conn, Stein (Henderson),
MacDonald A., Johnston. **Attendance: 30,000**

30 September, 1st Round, 2nd Leg
V Bayern Munich (Home) 1-1
McCloy, Jardine, Miller, Greig, McKinnon,
Jackson (Johnstone), Fyfe (Henderson),
Conn, Stein (1), MacDonald A., Johnston.
Attendance: 82,743

SCOTTISH FA CUP

23 January, 3rd Round
V Falkirk (Home) 3-0
McCloy, Jardine, Mathieson, Greig,
McKinnon, Jackson, Henderson, Conn (1),
Stein, Smith, Johnston (2).
Attendance: 42,000

13 February, 4th Round
V St Mirren (Away) 3-1
McCloy, Jardine, Mathieson, Greig,
McKinnon, Jackson, Henderson, Conn,
Stein (2), Smith, Johnston (1 pen).
Attendance: 32,373

6 March, 5th Round
V Aberdeen (Home) 1-0
McCloy, Jardine, Mathieson, Greig,
McKinnon, Jackson (1), Henderson, Conn
(MacDonald A.), Stein, Smith, Johnston.
Attendance: 60,584

31 March, Semi-Final
V Hibernian (Hampden Park) 0-0
McCloy, Jardine, Mathieson, Greig,
McKinnon, Jackson, Henderson, Conn,
Stein, MacDonald A., Johnston.
Attendance: 69,429

5 April, Semi-Final Replay
V Hibernian (Hampden Park) 2-1
McCloy, Jardine, Mathieson, Greig,
McKinnon, Jackson, Henderson (1),
MacDonald A., Stein, Conn (1), Johnston.
Attendance: 54,435

9 May, Final
V Celtic (Hampden Park) 1-1
McCloy, Miller, Mathieson, Greig,
McKinnon, Jackson, Henderson, Penman
(Johnstone (1)), Stein, MacDonald A.,
Johnston. **Attendance: 120,092**

12 May, Final Replay
V Celtic (Hampden Park) 1-2
Callaghan (og)
McCloy, Denny, Mathieson, Greig,
McKinnon, Jackson, Henderson, Penman,
Stein, MacDonald A., Johnston.
Attendance: 103,332

Scottish League Cup

8 August, Section 2 Game
V Dunfermline Athletic (Home) 4-1
Watson B., Jardine (1), Mathieson, Greig,
McKinnon, Smith, Henderson, Conn,
Stein (2), MacDonald A., Johnston (1 pen).
Attendance: 45,056

12 August, Section 2 Game
V Motherwell (Away) 2-0
McCloy, Jardine, Mathieson (Miller), Greig,
McKinnon, Jackson, Henderson (1), Conn,
Stein, Fyfe (1), Johnston. **Attendance: 25,000**

15 August, Section 2 Game
V Morton (Home) 0-0
McCloy, Jardine, Miller, Greig, McKinnon,
Jackson, Henderson, Conn, Stein, Fyfe,
Johnston (MacDonald A.).
Attendance: 45,000

19 August, Section 2 Game
V Motherwell (Home) 2-0
McCloy, Jardine, Miller, Greig, McKinnon,
Jackson, Henderson, Penman (1), Stein (1),
Johnston, McDonald I. (Conn).
Attendance: 35,000

22 August, Section 2 Game
V Dunfermline Athletic (Away) 6-0
McCloy, Jardine, Miller, Greig, McKinnon,
Jackson (1), Fyfe (1), Conn, Stein (1),
MacDonald A., Johnston (3 (1 pen)).
Attendance: 17,000

26 August, Section 2 Game
V Morton (Away) 2-0
McCloy, Jardine, Miller, Conn (1),
McKinnon, Jackson, Fyfe, Semple, Stein,
MacDonald A., Johnston (1).
Attendance: 18,000

Section 2 Group Table

	Played	Won	Drawn	Lost	F	A	Points
Rangers	6	5	1	0	16	1	11
Morton	6	3	1	2	8	8	7
Motherwell	6	2	1	3	8	8	5
Dumferline Athletic	6	0	1	5	4	19	1

9 September, Quarter Final, 1st Leg
V Hibernian (Away) 3-1
McCloy, Jardine, Miller, Greig, McKinnon,
Jackson, Stein, Fyfe (2), Johnston, Conn (1),
MacDonald A. **Attendance: 37,365**

23 September, Quarter Final, 2nd Leg
V Hibernian (Home) 3-1
McCloy, Jardine, Miller, Greig (1),
McKinnon, Jackson, Fyfe (1), Conn, Stein,
MacDonald A. (1), Johnston (Henderson).
Attendance: 54,000

14 October, Semi-Final
V Cowdenbeath (Hampden Park) 2-0
McCloy, Jardine, Miller, Greig, McKinnon,
Jackson, Henderson, Conn, Stein (1),
MacDonald A., Johnston (1 pen).
Attendance: 35,000

24 October, Final
V Celtic (Hampden Park) 1-0
McCloy, Jardine, Miller, Conn, McKinnon,
Jackson, Henderson, MacDonald A.,
Johnstone (1), Stein, Johnston.
Attendance: 106,263

Glasgow Cup Final

10 August
V Celtic (Hampden Park) 1-3
Watson B., Jardine, Mathieson, Greig (1),
Jackson, Smith, Henderson, Conn, Stein,
MacDonald A., Johnston. **Attendance: 58,144**

APPENDIX 2

Rangers Appearances 1970/71

Player	Lge	EFC	SC	LC	Total
Tom Alexander	2	0	0	0	2
Alfie Conn	22+2	2	5	9+1	38+3
Jim Denny	0	0	1	0	1
Graham Fyfe	12+3	2	0	6	20+3
John Greig	27	2	7	8	44
Willie Henderson	29	0+2	7	6+1	42+3
Colin Jackson	34	2	7	9	52
Sandy Jardine	33	2	5	10	50
Willie Johnston	25	2	7	10	44
Derek Johnstone	13+4	0+1	0+1	1	14+6
Willie Mathieson	14	0	7	2	23
Alex Miller	21	2	1	8+1	32+1
Angus McCallum	1	0	0	0	1
Peter McCloy	31	2	7	9	49
Alex MacDonald	27+6	2	4+1	7+1	40+8
Iain McDonald	3	0	0	1	4
Don McKinnon	32	2	7	10	51
Gerry Neef	3	0	0	0	3
Derek Parlane	2+2	0	0	0	2+2
Andy Penman	3+4	0	2	1	6+4
Billy Semple	1	0	0	1	2
Dave Smith	8+2	0	3	1	12+2
Colin Stein	30	2	7	10	49
Bobby Watson	0	0	0	1	1
Kenny Watson	1	0	0	0	1

Rangers Goalscorers 1970/71

Player	Lge	EFC	SC	LC	Total
Colin Stein	12	1	2	5	20
Willie Johnston	9	0	3	6	18
John Greig	8	0	0	1	9
Derek Johnstone	6	0	1	1	8
Alfie Conn	4	0	2	2	8
Graham Fyfe	3	0	0	5	8
Alex MacDonald	6	0	0	1	7
Willie Henderson	3	0	1	1	5
Colin Jackson	2	0	1	1	4
Sandy Jardine	1	0	0	1	2
Willie Mathieson	1	0	0	0	1
Alex Miller	1	0	0	0	1
Andy Penman	0	0	0	1	1
Own Goals	2	0	1	0	3

Appendix 3

Top six positions in Scottish League Division 1 **before** 2 January 1971.

Pos	Team	P	W	D	L	F	A	Pts
1	Aberdeen	19	16	2	1	45	7	34
2	Celtic	18	15	1	2	42	8	31
3	St Johnstone	19	10	4	5	36	28	24
4	Rangers	19	10	3	6	36	19	23
5	Falkirk	19	8	6	5	24	20	22
6	Dundee	19	8	5	6	29	24	21

Top six positions in Scottish League Division 1 **after** 2 January 1971.

Pos	Team	P	W	D	L	F	A	Pts
1	Aberdeen	20	17	2	1	46	7	36
2	Celtic	19	15	2	2	43	9	32
3	Rangers	20	10	4	6	37	20	24
4	St Johnstone	20	10	4	6	36	29	24
5	Falkirk	19	8	6	5	24	20	22
6	Dundee	19	8	5	6	29	24	21

Final positions in Scottish League Division 1 at **end of season** 1970/71.

Pos	Team	P	W	D	L	F	A	Pts
1	Celtic	34	25	6	3	89	23	56
2	Aberdeen	34	24	6	4	68	18	54
3	St Johnstone	34	19	6	9	59	44	44
4	Rangers	34	16	9	9	58	34	41
5	Dundee	34	14	10	10	53	45	38
6	Dundee Utd	34	14	8	12	53	54	36
7	Falkirk	34	13	9	12	46	53	35
8	Morton	34	13	8	13	44	44	34
9	Airdrie	34	13	8	13	60	65	34
10	Motherwell	34	13	8	13	43	47	34
11	Hearts	34	13	7	14	41	40	33
12	Hibernian	34	10	10	14	47	53	30
13	Kilmarnock	34	10	8	16	43	67	28
14	Ayr United	34	9	8	17	37	54	26
15	Clyde	34	8	10	16	33	59	26
16	Dunfernline	34	6	11	17	44	56	23
17	St Mirren	34	7	9	18	38	56	23
18	Cowdenbeath	34	7	3	24	33	77	17

2nd JANUARY 1971
BRYAN TODD
ROBERT McADAM
PETER WRIGHT
JOHN GARDINER
RICHARD BARK
WILLIAM THOMSON SUMMERHILL
GEORGE ADAMS
JOHN NEIL
JAMES TRAINER